<u>REAL ESTATE 3.0</u>

*Use The Internet To Sell Your Home And Stop
Paying Commissions To Obsolete Real Estate Agents!*

REAL ESTATE 3.0

*Use The Internet To Sell Your Home And Stop
Paying Commissions To Obsolete Real Estate Agents!*

James Joseph

New York

Real Estate 3.0
Using the Internet to Sell Your Home and
Stop Paying Commissions to an Obsolete Agent

ISBN 978-1-60037-606-1

Library of Congress Control Number: 2009927683

Cover Design by: Rachel Lopez rachel@r2cdesign.com

MORGAN · JAMES
THE ENTREPRENEURIAL PUBLISHER

Morgan James Publishing, LLC
1225 Franklin Ave., STE 325
Garden City, NY 11530-1693
Toll Free 800-485-4943
www.MorganJamesPublishing.com

In an effort to support local communities, raise awareness and funds, Morgan James Publishing donates one percent of all book sales for the life of each book to Habitat for Humanity. Get involved today, visit **www.HelpHabitatForHumanity.org.**

This book is dedicated to the four women
I admire and love the most.
Alice, Ellen, Zan and Stephanie.

ACKNOWLEDGEMENTS

To my amazing mother, Alice – she is the greatest power of example and strength that a guy has ever been blessed with. I truly question whether I would still be here if it were not for your love and genius.

To Mary Casey, Esq. Thank you for your friendship, help, generosity and guidance. You have my complete confidence.

To my big brother Chris Knuth and his terrific wife Shaunna who have always been there for me. If there were more people in the world as sincere as you both are the world would certainly be a better place to live in.

To my brother John and sister Ellen - I love you and would not change a thing. Thank you for your support.

To my friend Marina Giovannini- thank you for all your time and effort that has made this book possible.

Special thanks to Bob Proctor whose Secret Cruise became my inspiration to write this book and to Alex Mandossian who has been the voice of guidance.

To Bill Wilson for the life that he and his amazing boss have given me.

Thank you Bob Russell for all your help and creativity.

To Stephanie my best friend and spiritual partner. Without your love, encouragement, coaching, enthusiasm, support and patience it would not have been possible for me to have completed this book. I love you. We are living our dreams and this is just the beginning!

Contents

Acknowledgements. vii

Introduction xiii

Online xv

PART I The "Current Conflict System" 1

What the Real Estate Industry Does Not Want You to Know 3

History of the Problem – The Original System. 5

The Present Conflict System 11

More Conflicts and Less Representation 13

Dual agency "Double Agent" 14

Revolution is the Solution 17

Buyer's Agents 19

In the Best Interest of Whom 22

Opposing Interest 27

Multiple Listing Service 30

    Days on Market. 31

    Original Asking Price 32

    Average Selling Price 33

    Average Selling Price per Square Foot 34

    Withheld Information 35

Multiple Listing Service Forms. 38

    Seller's Statement of Condition (Property Disclosure Form). . 39

    Deposit Money Conflicts 44

    Agency Disclosure. 46

    The Commission Mystery. 48

PART II The Way To Change. 55

Commission Comparisons 57

Anticipated Seller Expenses 61

12 Principles for Successful Internet Real Estate Selling. 63

    Principle 1. Be Brave And Set The Price 69

    Principle 2. Perform Inspections Before Marketing 75

    Principle 3. Represent The Exact Condition of The Property . 78

    Principle 4. Hire an Attorney. 80

    Principle 5. Proof of Insurance 86

    Principle 6. Anything You Say Will Be used Against You . . . 89

    Principle 7. Pay Buyers Brokers. 92

    Principle 8. Sell Directly To Buyers Without Agents 94

    Principle 9. Internet Advertising is Cheap 96

    Principle 10. Showings Are Easy 106

    Principle 11. Follow Up. 110

    Principle 12. All Info About Property Stays With Property . 114

Example of OFFER TO PURCHASE 116

Example of PURCHASE AND SALE AGREEMENT 120

PART III Other Advice. 129

End of the Information Dinosaur 131

The Black Hole. 133

Financing 135

Pre-Qualification Letters 136

Pre-Approval Letters 137

Commitment Letters. 138

Deposits 139

Amount of Good Faith Deposit 141

Signs 143

Holding Your Own Open House. 145

Old photos. 147

Final Walk Through 148

PART IV Real Estate 3.0 151

www.FreeRealEstateOffice.com 153

Seller's Offices 155

Buyer's Offices 160

Conference Room/Negotiating Table 164

Transaction Department 166

Closing Table 168

Unique Feature. 170

INTRODUCTION

Desperately attempting to keep its tentacles attached to and controlling of the Real Estate industry in America, the National Association of Realtors (NAR) has converted to a system that is rife with problems and conflict of interest. Although The National Association of Realtors members spend a great amount of energy claiming to be the savior and supporter of ethics, their main mission is and has always been all about self-preservation.

Many of the existing conflict of interest issues are the result of poor decisions that the National Association of Realtors has made, placing its interests of buyers above those of the sellers. There is no other explanation. Whenever the two interests are at odds, it seems it is always the sellers who lose more ground. The National Association of Realtors is an enormous group that claims it maintains a strong fiduciary relationship with the sellers of America, but its actions show otherwise.

In the 1990's Bill Gates challenged the National Association of Realtors. In his 1996 book, "The Road Ahead", Bill Gates predicted that the Internet would change "the whole system of real estate agencies and commissions." This is because buyers and sellers would have direct access to so much information that the way real estate is sold would change. Typically, the National Association of Realtors rallied full force to maintain its stronghold on the marketplace without taking into consideration that this man's presence might have an enormous positive influence on real estate technologies. Once again, the NAR went on the defensive for the sake of its own self-preservation.

In all fairness, pull up www.realtor.com and take a good look at what the National Association of Realtors and the Multiple Listing Service (MLS) offers sellers for technology and modern information sharing and systems. Just short of nothing. This website is a dinosaur of an excuse for an Internet site when you compare it to what your children are using to amuse themselves online. All that is provided to a seller on the website for technology is the same view that anyone else can get on www.realtor.com. How is it that in this society, made up of the very people who make, design and run the leading edge technology industries, sellers are satisfied with the mundane, minuscule offering of a single property information page and some jpeg images of our real estate on www.realtor.com? Most Americans have more technology in their homes than what the NAR shares with them to sell those same homes.

The focus is the problem. Focus is the very reason why Mr. Gates real estate site has not successfully challenged the NAR. His focus, like so many others, is exactly the same at the NAR. They all cater to the real estate buyers of the world and not the sellers.

This book and www.FreeRealEstateOffice.com have the opposite focus. This system has been exclusively designed for the sellers of the world. The sellers and property owners are the overlooked and forgotten class that shall receive the benefit of a free Internet sales system that is light years ahead of the dinosaur that the NAR calls www.realtor.com .

I agree that Bill Gates was partially correct about the future of real estate marketing. The Internet has replaced the need for selling and listing agents. Their services are obsolete and conflicting at best.

Real estate agents are representing buyers on the one side and now www.FreeRealEstateOffice.com represents sellers on the other. Technology and up to the minute information sharing on www. FreeRealEstateOffice.com and its features streamline the entire process, from pricing to closing. It assists the seller to actually market and complete the sales process online. It is the wave of the future and that wave is here and now.

A much-needed revolution to change the current conflict system of selling your real estate is here. A system designed entirely for you -- the sellers and owners of real property. Our system is steeped in everything technology has to offer and saves sellers thousands of dollars in unnecessary commission expenses.

ONLINE

It is a fact that most real estate buyers looking for property search for it over the Internet.

It is a well kept secret that advertising on line is actually dirt-cheap!

Some of the largest regional newspapers have online advertising rates of just $99.00 for a three-month online advertisement. Compare these rates to one month of print advertising in the same newspaper and you will soon understand that the cost of going online is the deal of the century.

This book will not only show you how to sell your property saving the enormous commission expense of a listing broker, but also how to easily utilize and take full advantage of online newspaper advertising, free Internet listing sites together with the www.FreeRealEstateOffice. com you can replace listing brokers!

Placing your property information onto www.FreeRealEstateOffice. com is done similar to an Ebay submission. After this, it is usually very simple to just download the format onto whatever online newspaper site makes sense for the seller to advertise with.

The www.FreeRealEstateOffice.com is a complete sales system to enable sellers and property owners to pre-market, market, negotiate, track banking, contingencies, schedule and manage the closing of their transaction.

The sales component of the system advises and guides you through the sales process including resources such as referrals, contracts, agreements, supplies and sales principals.

The www.FreeRealEstateOffice.com system will allow Sellers

access to never before available tools like instant buyer interest/inquiry notification. Finance tracking is included so contingencies are always updated and worthwhile. Also instantly binding deposits are available through www.FreeRealEstateOffice.com.

Information sharing and real time communications with everyone involved in the transaction take the mystery and frustration out of the sale. On line negotiations and agreements are performed on the www.FreeRealEstateOffice.com system so as to distance and protect the Seller.

Everything that can be provided for online in a real estate transaction is included on www.FreeRealEstateOffice.com. Through this system the entire transaction, from pricing to closing, can easily be accomplished.

PART I

The "current conflict system"

WHAT THE REAL ESTATE INDUSTRY
DOES NOT WANT YOU TO KNOW

In the 1990's a major shift occurred in the way the sellers of real estate were represented by real estate agents.

This change took place because major problems existed in the original system through which real estate was sold. In order to save money and protect themselves from liability, the National Association of Realtors and the insurance industry lobbied hard for this change.

What the real estate industry does not want the property owners and sellers of America to know is that this change and the new system it has created (that I have labeled "the conflict system") is worse for the sellers/owners of real estate in America. And, the real estate community has inflicted it upon you!

History of the Problem

The Original System

The original system of selling real estate had an enormous built-in problem called vicarious liability. For many years vicarious liability cost property sellers, agents and insurance companies millions, perhaps billions, of dollars paid out in damage awards.

Under the original system, all real estate agents worked for the seller through a technicality known as sub-agency. This meant that all agents had a fiduciary responsibility to the seller; Therefore under the old system all real estate agents worked in the best interest of the sellers. It is believed that the Multiple Listing Service itself created the existence of sub-agency to allow all Realtors*[1] the opportunity to sell each other's listings.

You would list your property with an agent, and all the other agents or offices that came with a buyer were supposedly working for and in the best interest of the seller. It did not matter if it was the listing agent or some stranger from four towns over that had a customer, every agent worked for the seller. At least in theory that was how it was supposed to work. There were no such entities as buyer agents. If an agent was

---

1   The term *REALTOR*® is a registered collective membership mark that identifies a real estate professional who is a member of the NATIONAL ASSOCIATION OF REALTORS® and subscribes to its **Code of Ethics**.

spending effort working with a buyer showing properties for sale, these agents were all supposedly working for the seller and never the buyer.

You can probably see where an agent could become attached to a buyer after spending months and months together looking at property. In most cases these agents did not know or perhaps never met the seller, but grew quite close to the buyers.

This is where things got problematic. Perhaps information was shared with the buyer that was counterproductive to the seller's best interest. This might have even included advice on negotiation strategies.

What happened back then is that the slightest misspoken words, mistake, misrepresentation or incorrect answer, real or intentional, set off a chain reaction.

Oh sure, as the Seller you didn't do anything wrong! You had never met the buyers or the buyer's real estate agent. You were never even present for the showings.

Under the old system of representation it did not matter! All the agents worked for the seller and vicarious liability would ensure that the aggrieved party (the buyer) could and would sue everyone involved who had any money including the seller.

So let's take a look at an example of a sale gone badly under the old system.

In the following example of a sale, there are two agents from two different real estate offices involved in the same transaction because it was a co-brokered sale. The house was listed with Jane Doe who works for ABC realty and the selling agent was John Smith from XYZ Realty who showed the property and had the buyer. The buyer now desires to file a lawsuit. Lets say for misrepresentation concerning the age of the roof. So just what are the buyer's chances of success in this lawsuit?

Potential Lawsuit Targets

Lawsuits follow the money!

1. The seller is a prime target because they have money from the sale.
2. The seller's listing office - ABC Realty
3. The broker at ABC Realty
4. The seller's listing agent - Jane Doe

5. The insurance Company for ABC realty
6. The insurance company for Jane Doe
7. The co-broke office – XYZ Realty
8. The broker at XYZ Realty
9. The co-broke agent – John Smith
10. The insurance company for XYZ Realty
11. The insurance company for John Smith

There would be **11 Clear targets** for possible involvement in a lawsuit.

And all this could have happened because John Smith spoke out of turn and mislead the buyer about the roof without the seller or the sellers agent having had the slightest part in the discussion about the roof. Yet they were all liable for the damages.

With 11 targets the chance of the buyer getting paid by someone or a combination or many was very high.

Now let's compound this example a little further and saying that this property was shown 10 times and by 10 different offices.

Do the math again:

11   Different entities that could have potentially made an error. The listing agent (Jane Doe) and 10 other complete strangers now equals 11 different entities.

X11   Times 11 different targets to potentially file a lawsuit in this co- brokered sale

= 121   **different opportunities have been created for a potential lawsuit.**

By having strangers working for the seller, under the old system of representation, it created 121 different liability situations and this was only from showing the house 10 times!

The most frightening thing about this crazy system of liability roulette was that it was the seller who never had insurance coverage to protect him/her against the potential lawsuit and that the seller had a definite amount of known cash from the sale to loose. Any losses always came out of the seller's pocket. The others involved usually had insurance to protect them.

Was this a great system? I think not! Get yourself sued because an agent who is a complete stranger to you and perhaps now on very friendly terms with the buyer makes a misrepresentation. One stranger (the sub-agent co-broker) tells another stranger (the buyer) that perhaps your roof is in good shape when it is actually 30 years old and needs replacement or, maybe the agent says something like the back lot line is at least 75 feet in the rear of the house, when in fact it is actually only 20 feet away. Now the new buyer can never install a much dreamt of in-ground pool. Who do you think was always a target of these lawsuits? The Seller!

The bottom line is vicarious liability went on way too long and needed to be avoided. It was costing everyone involved far too much money. The real estate agents and offices were taking a big hit. The insurance companies were making error and omissions insurance harder and harder to obtain and sellers were taking a real financial beating.

So what did the National Association of Realtors come up with?

They created the new and improved **"Conflict System"** that exists today.

They distanced themselves from the liability problem they created and from the sellers. This **"Conflict System"** has resulted is the complete sell-out of the property owners and sellers in favor of the buyers. The system was supposedly established to protect the sellers, but in fact, the only ones who have insulated themselves from liability is the vast number of agents who created the problem in the first place.

The Realtors and agents were all getting too close to the buyers and The National Association of Realtors and their insurers all knew it. So they changed the rules to form a new system where that relationship is perfectly acceptable. As long as the seller does not pay the buyers agent, the buyer's agents do not work for the seller and there does not now exist the sub-agency problems of the past. Presently the conflict does not exist as far as the Realtors and government agencies are concerned.

The only catch is that currently the seller in most transactions still pays for the buyer's agent. They just treat the entire class of sellers as if they are less than bright and tell the sellers they are not paying for the services of the buyer's agent, when in fact they almost always pay every agent involved in their transaction. Legal bait and switch!

So the agents do not work for the seller but more often the not they are still paid by the seller.

THE PRESENT CONFLICT FILLED SYSTEM

So now the pendulum has swung to the extreme opposite side.

The real estate community has bailed out on full representation of the property owners and sellers of America.

Before the change, under the original system, all the agents were working in the **best interest of the seller.** Now with the present "conflict system," most of the agents work in the **best interest of the buyer.** An agent that is working in the **best interest of a buyer** means that this agent's responsibility is to obtain a certain parcel of real estate for the very least amount of money and under the very best of terms for that buyer. This is a completely opposing interest to the **seller's best interest.** Which is to make the most amount of money for the property and with terms completely favorable to the seller.

As far as commissions are concerned, the "**conflict system**" is much the same in that the sellers usually pay for all the agents involved in the transaction. What has changed is that this includes paying the buyers agents. The sellers pay the people working **against their best interest** – the buyer's agents. The twisted explanation given as to who pays who is a real sidewinder and it goes something like this. The buyer's agent works for the buyer and is paid by the buyer, but it comes out of the seller's money. Basically the seller pays even though they tell you the seller does not pay. A 5% commission out of the seller's proceeds at closing is still a 5% commission out of the seller's proceeds regardless of whether it took place in 1985 under the original system, or last week under the "**conflict system.**" That's right, they have twisted the way things are worded, but the reality is the seller usually still pays the entire commission. This is the same way commission splits between the selling office and listing office have always been handled; only now the fiduciary capacities have completely changed.

This is another self-serving situation where the industry has entirely changed the formula except for the formula as to who and how they get paid. Regardless of the **conflict of interest** it now creates. The industry continues to create this conflict of interest while spreading the good word about fiduciary responsibility. I still do not know how they sold this grand deception to America!

The Association of Realtors, Inc. has a form known as an **Exclusive Right to Represent Buyer** form. This form states, "The broker will make every effort to obtain payment of all or any part of this fee by the seller of the property." The fee this pertains to is the "professional services fee" also known as the buyer's agent commission.

Here is an Association of Realtors, Inc. form that gives instructions as to how someone working counter productive to the seller's best interest will also try to be paid by that same seller. It is kind of like, don't worry about the money, I'll get the seller to pay me if I can and, oh by the way, not only will I try to accomplish this, I am also going to try to get them to take less money for their property as well. So they are going to try and take advantage of you and get paid by you for doing it. And the real estate community set this system up. That's right! You read it correctly, no need to go back and re-read it because it didn't make much sense the first time through.

In the Multiple Listing Forms, seller's agents inform buyer's agents how much of the commission they are prepared to share or pay the buyers agent. So here is the true test. Who is paying the buyers agent? The seller is paying the buyers agent, but the seller is told that the seller is not paying the buyers agent. Doesn't this sound like something that has come straight out of Washington D.C.?

More Conflicts and Less Representation

Do you know that if you list your property for sale with one of the major office/franchises – let's say a big one with 100 agents or more – only one agent in the entire company is now supposedly working for you. You pull up to their big fancy office building and close – very, very close to everyone working inside that office is working for the other guy (the Buyer).

What about the management at this fine office? Who do they work for? Is it 99% buyer's management and 1% seller's management? Are they working in the best interest of the company? Are they working in the best interest of their agents? Are they neutral representing no one's best interest?

You need to be extremely careful in this environment. Anything you say or do could be used against you. This is not a joke. A good buyer's agent has the legal obligation to report information and facts to his/her clients that can be useful.

For instance, while you are interviewing a potential seller's agent for your needs, other agents in that office overhear the fact that you lost your job and need to sell due to financial pressures. These other agents have the responsibility to give this information to a potential buyer if it will help the potential buyer.

Dual Agent/"Double Agent"

Here is another conflicting situation that creates the Holy Grail for a real estate agent. This is a phenomenon known as **Dual Agency.** Also known as getting both sides of the deal, or what I have labeled as becoming a **"Double Agent."** The reason this is so sought after is that agents basically double their commission on a transaction by working as both a buyer's agent and a seller's agent at the same time.

A seller hires an agent to represent his or her best interest. This agent finds a buyer directly for the seller's property with no other agent involved. The agent will now double his or her income by working for both parties, collecting the entire commission. This double agent now works basically for no one and everyone all at the same time. In order to avoid a conflict of interest, this agent must remain completely neutral and become a facilitator of the transaction.

In all actuality, this is impossible. No one is capable of working for two opposing sides of interests in any transaction. Have you ever heard of a dual attorney? Of course not! It simply cannot be done. Once again, the real estate industry has self-servingly twisted the situation around for its own best interest and created this phenomenon only allowed in the real estate community.

What they do to supposedly avoid this conflict of interest is to step back and become neutral, a facilitator of the transaction. The agent theoretically avoids the dispensing of any information to either side that could be confidential and used to the others advantage.

So the bottom line is that your agent gets to bail out on you and in doing so, double his or her income. This is entirely and only in the agent's best interest. Where is the fiduciary responsibility now that he or she can make more money and from you? You were the very entity they were sworn to protect.

Let's say you're a seller of a $500,000 house, paying a 5% or $25,000 commission. For $25,000, don't you want, deserve and haven't you paid for every drop of information that could help you get all $500,000 and not a penny less if at all avoidable? You will not get all the information you need or were privy to, if you agent becomes a facilitator. Your ability to negotiate has been diminished by someone you trusted who now has left you at a very critical moment, at the point of negotiations with a buyer, which is one of the reasons you were paying for representation in the first place.

This agent has left your side and expects an increase in pay. And you are the one expected to pay it. What about your money? Who else cares now? The agent gets more for less and the seller gets less for more.

The act of real estate agents changing from their fiduciary responsibility of full representation of the seller, to neutral a position, all the while advancing themselves financially should become a chargeable offense – a crime!

How do they claim to maintain a fiduciary capacity of any kind to the seller when their ultimate goal is entirely in their own best interest as evidenced by this scam of a self-centered move?

Under the original system, agents could receive all of the commission and still maintain their fiduciary responsibility, but in this present "conflict system", it is impossible.

Manipulating this unworkable situation for the best interest of the agents is all that has been achieved.

Let's go back to the large franchise office I mentioned earlier and consider that you listed your property for sale with them. Complete this scenario using the above described double agent situation.

Of the total 100 agents and management, 99 of the agents work entirely in the best interest of buyers. Make no mistake about it. Their job is to help a buyer pay as small an amount as possible for your property. To help their buyers save money is to take money out of the seller's pocket. Management is either there in the best interest of the company, the agents, or perhaps is neutral to your cause. The agent you hired has declared that he is working as a double agent. He or she is working in his or her best interest and neutral to your cause.

Out of more than 100 people in that office, sadly, **no one is working in your best interest!** Why are you paying these people thousands of dollars and what they are accomplishing for you? The fact remains the real estate community as a whole is working in the buyer's best interest.

Compare this to a football game. You have the ball 1st and 10 on the 10 yard line and you are ready to score. You look up from the middle of the huddle only to realize that you are standing there with only your quarterback. Everyone else on the team has gone and all the rules have changed. Your entire team, coaches, managers, cheerleaders everyone even the water boy and equipment personnel have switched sides and they have all moved across the field to the opposing sides' bench.

Your chance to score has now been sorely diminished. But wait, it gets even worse because now your quarterback informs you that he can go neutral and he is going to go neutral right now. And by the way you are now going to double his already huge salary by standing there and allowing him to facilitate both the offence and the defense.

Everything has changed with the exception of the huge commission expense that sellers still pay out for shrinking representation.

Sellers, you are all but alone on the ball field. It has been done to you. Very quietly and very surely, this change over to the **"conflict system"** has been installed with all sorts of self-justification for poor behavior by realtors and agents.

REVOLUTION IS THE SOLUTION

The Evolution of the Real Estate 3.0 System of Seller Representation

The real estate community has dramatically changed its relationship with us, now it is time to change our relationship with it!

The solution is simple! End Seller's agency and save at least ½ of the commission. The real estate industry has completely changed everything over to a buyer-centered market. We need to follow their lead and even go one step further. It is time for a third generation of Seller representation. It is time for the creation of Real Estate 3.0 which is Seller self-representation over the Internet.

We need to emulate the way the industry is concentrating on the buyers and buyer's agents and stop the use of listing agents and selling agents.

Stop using seller's agents. We do not need them. In many ways, they have become detrimental and obsolete to our cause and much too expensive for what they offer.

Save the entire half of the commission that you would have paid a listing agent and use your money far more effectively to market your property online.

It is not the buyer's agents that are the problem. Buyer's agency is very worthwhile and a good practice if it is kept completely separate from the seller's agency.

It is the seller's agents and their co-mingling of responsibilities that has created this problem as well as many others. Sellers agents are confused about just whom they work for. One minute it's the seller, the next minute it's both the buyer and seller (neutral) and the next moment they are working strictly for themselves. When this particular conflict doesn't exist, there are many others that put you at risk. We need to put a stop to all this confusion that costs us more money, creating problems and conflict. What we need to do is end the poor seller representation that has been taking place and stop using seller's agents.

Real Estate 3.0 considers every agent a buyer's agent. No more listing and selling agents, their services are costly, obsolete and no longer needed. Only Buyer agents are to be utilized. This surely puts an end to the confusion and conflict.

The selling agents do not concentrate on buyers, and when they do procure a buyer for that same master, it places that relationship in complete conflict and this is when the seller's agent bails out on their fiduciary capacity with you anyway. This is no longer to be tolerated.

BUYER'S AGENTS

Copy the market shift and concentrate on the buyers and the buyer agents. They have exactly what we need.

Although their interests are completely divergent, the common denominator between seller and buyer is the property. Separate and protect those interests while cooperating and concentrating on the sale is the goal.

This is NOT for sale by owner (FSBO). **This is Real Estate 3.0.** For sale by owner has generally excluded all agents. We encourage cooperation and payment of buyer's agents. To exclude buyer's agents the way traditional FSBO does is a very foolish decision.

With all the legal ramifications of the "do not call lists", many agents are instructed by their offices not to approach FSBO's for fear of legal prosecution and fines. Why would anyone choose to alienate this group that represents the single largest pool of buyers in the marketplace? FSBO'S are usually fairly radical independent types that want to be left alone to do his or her thing. That is his/her decision, but that is not what we are all about. Real Estate 3.0 requires cooperation with the buyer's agents.

Real Estate 3.0 takes the opposite viewpoint from the FSBO attitude. We respect, recognize and support the buyer's agent's relationship in our process. Our system requires the cooperation and compensation to buyer agents. Only properties that offer buyer agent compensation are accepted from our sellers. So, any and all properties on our system will work with buyer's agents. Full advanced disclosure of the commission amount is boldly displayed on the property information page for the whole world to see. There is absolutely no reason to keep commissions a secret. Buyer agents do not need to be members of the National Association of Realtors or any Multiple Listing Service. What will be required prior to showing a property is documentation that the agent is licensed in good standing for that particular state and can show proof of sufficient error and omissions insurance?

The scheduling for showings is easy and done directly with the property owner. Be it by phone, email or the unique property code through the system and signage. The seller has elected his or her best way to communicate. How much more efficient is this compared to the way buyer's agents have always needed to go through multiple layers of people in order to set up a single showing. And keep in mind the buyer's agent never has to worry again if the selling agent is playing games as to whether the property is actually still available or not. They now shall receive an answer directly from the owner. There are no other agents in the middle of communications to be suspicious of.

As a protection for the seller, the only direct contact between the seller and the buyer's agent will be at the property viewing and this is also at the seller's discretion as well. **Principal #6** coaches sellers to limit their conversation about the property. The use of the lockbox entry system will still be employed if the seller wishes. For the protection, ease and comfort of the seller, our system will require that all negotiations take place only online. Our system has a great format for the submission of offers, agreements and contracts. This will enable all involved parties, throughout the entire transaction, to have complete up to the minute information status reports.

Buyer's agents are realty professionals and they are not allowed to negotiate directly with the seller. We cannot and will not allow agents to obtain the upper hand in negotiations. A level playing field is established if separation is maintained. If any direct communication is necessary, with the seller's permission, the seller's legal counsel can be contacted.

Under the current **"conflict System"** sellers depend on information and updates by the trickle down or chain reaction communication system. That is, if a seller wants to know the status of any number of issues, lets say for instance how the buyer's financing is progressing, a chain reaction of up to eight phone calls needs to be successfully made to obtain an answer to this one very basic and critical question. This smoke signal form of communication is now a thing of the past. On the www.FreeRealEstateOffice.com any and all information and communication, starting with inspection reports and continuing through mortgage, legal and closing information is located online in the property filing cabinet. Instead of waiting for days for a return phone call, simply go to your property filing cabinet for a real time update at any time.

Under this system, there is only one agent (the buyer's agent) involved in any given transaction. This will be the end of commission games and fights. The commission is clearly posted on the property information sheet and paid at the transfer of the deed.

Our sellers can, of course, sell direct to a buyer without a buyer's agent involvement. In these cases, un-represented buyers need to declare their status before a showing is performed in order to avoid any conflict with the agent community.

Any property on our system can easily be viewed by the world. Pull up the page and look, it's that simple. Be it land, houses or commercial property. Unlike some of the other listing services, there is no registration page, hidden information such as addresses or lengthy membership and fees required before viewing. This has created barriers to potential buyers is totally unnecessary. We want to sell property, not steer buyers to particular agents by keeping secrets that can only be unlocked by them. Pull up the page and search. It's as simple as that.

Follow the **12 SALES PRINCIPLES FOR SUCCESSFUL INTERNET PROPERTY SELLING** and you will be able to sell and cooperate with buyers agents, while saving the half of the commission that you would have wasted on a listing agent.

In the Best Interest of Whom?

All real estate agents have a fiduciary relationship/responsibility to someone. This means that they legally and ethically need to place someone else's interest above all others – even their own.

Under the old system, they almost exclusively worked in the seller's best interest. This meant that above all factors they should all have been working to get the highest price in the least amount of time with a minimum amount of negative exposure for every seller on the market.

Now the vast majority of agents have a fiduciary responsibility to the buyer.

This means that above many factors, most agents work in the best interest of the buyer.

It is a buyer's agent's responsibility to help a buyer pay the very least amount of money for a piece of property.

The seller, simply put, is second-class. It's all about the buyer and what they can save and how they can benefit at the seller's expense.

This is a monumental change.

It is impossible to serve two masters, so why is it common for real estate agents to serve three?

Back in the 90's all of the real estate agents were on your team. They were on your side of the equation, as professionals, watching out for your best interest! And it was commonplace that the sellers were getting sued.

Now almost all of them have gone over to the dark side. They have switched teams. Even though it is still your money that pays them, they now work against you. So this system does not work well for the seller either.

Real Estate 3.0 represents the third change in the system that is meant to work for the seller.

Let's say you decide or need to sell your real property and are not sure which agent to hire because you do not have any personal friendships with anyone in the real estate sales business.

You stop into a very large national office in the center of your town so that you might interview some potential agents. You step into an impressive building and enter into this real estate office's plush lobby.

Do you realize that, once you finish a harmless exchange of pleasantries with the receptionist, you are in financial trouble!

Yes, financial trouble. From this point on anything that you do or say can and will be used against you. Everyone who sees or hears you is potentially the enemy of your bank account. They are working for the other side as a buyer's agents.

Perhaps when you are greeted by a very knowledgeable professional realtor in the lobby as part of the introduction, you inform him or her that you are contemplating selling your property because you are divorcing and that you don't know exactly what your property is worth.

Anyone within ear shot, with only the exception of the agent you are talking with, (and this is only if you actually hire this agent), will use everything that you have just said against you, especially the part about the divorce.

Most offices only have one private conference room. You are fortunate this day because it is available and you can talk privately. If it weren't open for use, then all of your business would be available for the enemy to overhear – but this is your lucky day.

Walking to conference room, you make small talk, as strangers do, and the agent shares his or her empathy with you as they have also been divorced and he or she asks you a simple question – "how it is going?"

You answer "terrible." Now all the other buyer's agents know that you are in the middle of a terrible divorce and a terrible divorce usually means money or child visitation problems or both.

You go into the office and close the door and talk in private with your only potential ally in the entire building. I say potential ally because you have not hired this person so they do not work for you. Therefore, your future relationship is only a potential one.

After an exchange of information about you, your family situation, the property particulars, the agent's credentials and the company's fine marketing and support, you end your visit with an appointment for the agent to meet you at the property to discuss price.

You repeat this similar process at two other offices with which you would consider potentially listing your property.

Perhaps you have lived in town for several years and you and your spouse are fairly well known, through various activities – perhaps the kids and their sports or through organizations that the family supported.

Anyway, curious, perhaps even gossipy agents from town see you at their offices and inquire as to your situation.

Let's review how any of this might be in your best interest.

First, every office that you entered was completely full of spies. All these other agents and I literally mean all of them are working in opposition to your best interests. They are buyer's agents!

No one in the entire building is working for your best interest.

If you should hire the agent you meet with, then there is now one person supposedly with your best interest at heart. Only one realtor out of perhaps as many as fifty or more is on your side.

This agent will usually have a manager. In whose best interest is the manager working for? I am not sure.

The manager works directly for the company and the company is full of people working against your best interest. What are they to do? It is certainly unclear.

Your lack of complete privacy, in whose best interest was this? Everyone else's but yours. Not all of your conversations and information was protected. Is this your fault or the fault of the realty office? I blame the real estate office and companies. They should know better than to risk your information. A law firm would handle privileged information much differently. Why not a real estate firm?

You list your property for sale through one of the offices that you visited and there is also a high probability that a buyer's agent from one of these three offices will bring the buyer to your property. If any of these agents actually heard any privileged information during your meeting, these agents are OBLIGATED ethically and legally to inform their buyers as to any information that they might have that will help them secure a more favorable transaction for the Buyer. Obligated against your best interest and the kicker is that you are the one that told them and the realty office let you.

Now what about the other agents that you interviewed? You equally told all three of them your business. Perhaps you told them how tight money is now because you are paying for attorneys and you now have two separate sets of household expenses. Perhaps you told them what your bottom line price would be, and disclosed other personal information.

You can only hire one of these three agents that were interviewed to represent you. This leaves 2 people, 2 realtors who know all of your business and in the end you did not hire them. Is this in your best interest? Just in case you did not hire them, did you think ahead and have them sign some sort of confidentiality agreement, stating that they could not divulge any of your information to buyers or all their other agents in the office? Did their office provide you with such a form? Of course not, no office provides this kind of a non-disclosure protection for the seller but they obviously need to.

A few months go by and one of the two agents that you interviewed and did not list with has a potential buyer for your property and wants to show it.

Besides the fact that their ego is now damaged (and it usually will be so) because you did not hire them, do you think they will share with the Buyer all the inside information that you had shared with them? Yes. This insider information can and will now cost you money. They are obligated to share everything with the Buyer they represent. Is this in your best interest?

Now let's look at the fact that you publicly stated you are divorcing. Several people from town saw you and people like to gossip. Is it is your best interest that stories start and are spread through three different area offices that you **have** to sell you home because of a court order? Is this in your best interest?

What if we change the example a little bit? Instead of a divorce, you are transferring to another state for employment reasons. Or it's your mother's house and she has been confined to a nursing home because of poor health and the property is now a burden upon you, and your siblings don't provide any support. Perhaps it is your health. Let's say knee problems make it hard to climb stairs and all your bedrooms are on the second floor. Maybe it is severe money problems and you are trying to avoid foreclosure.

The list goes on and on. The point is that anything you say to the wrong real estate agent or realtor, and make no mistake -- 99.9% of them are the wrong person to confide in -- can and will be used against you for the benefit of the buyer.

Is this in your best interest? NO!

When realtors functioned under the original system, they all shared the same office space, shared the same managers, shared the same MLS information and statistics and it worked because they were on the same team, the seller's team.

Now under the present "conflict system," realtors still share the same office, share the same management, and have access the same MLS information and statistics, but it no longer works for the seller because they work for two opposing teams.

Everything and everybody is now co-mingled and it does not serve the seller well.

With the www.FreeRealEstateOffice.com information and interests are separate, as they should be.

Opposing Interest

Clearly sellers and buyers have distinct and opposite interests.

Therefore, seller's agents and buyer's agents have conflicting interests to serve.

Two groups have created the current **"Conflict System,"** namely The National Association of Realtors and The Multiple Listing Service.

Real estate agents and their associations have been permitted to self-servingly place their own interests before their committed interest to the sellers and owners of real estate.

The second reason that has created the current situation is that these same organizations and associations have never separated or segregated the information and systems from each other so that each interest can be truly protected.

The way it is presently, all the available information is now co-mingled. The opposing interest and information pertaining to buyers and sellers is being shared and mixed between both groups and with the wrong individuals. This is the current norm everywhere in modern day real estate sales and this practice needs to be stopped.

Serving the best interest of a seller or buyer and doing it well is a very worthy and difficult position to accomplish.

One of the problems is that most agents wear two hats. They want to list properties for sale and they want to sell properties to buyers. They work both ways. Their roles are very mixed and confusing at best. Real estate agents work for the seller one minute and work for a buyer the next.

Most real estate agents work in close proximity with many other agents. These Agents happen to work for both sellers and buyers as well.

Most know and try to get along with the other agents, not just in their office, in the entire region. First and foremost they talk and share with the other agents as individuals and maybe even as good friends.

Maybe, just maybe, they might consider whether the other agent is on your team (seller's) or the other team (buyer's). But, how is this accomplished and how are you guaranteed that the wrong information is not shared between them?

There is not much differentiation between your team (seller's) and that of the other team (buyer's). These agents sit together, share life's stories together, perhaps socialize together and have access to most of the same information together. MLS has made certain of this. So where is the dividing line?

There currently is not a division. For the sake of the sellers, there definitely needs to be a clear and certain separation between these groups that represent two distinct interests.

Let's take a quick look at typical real estate office meeting for agents. They usually take place at least once a week. In this particular example, the office has 20 agents and it takes place on any given Wednesday morning.

Surely the discussions shall center around what's sold, what's new by way of listings that past week and what's lingering on the market.

Any discussions that take place concerning your property between your listing agent and the other agents can be extremely detrimental to your best interest.

Do they openly discuss the fact that your property is priced too high? As a result does your listing agent suggest to you, the seller, that a price decrease is necessary? Or does your agent agree with the roomful of opinions and thereby confirm that ensuing offers for a lesser price are justified? This sets up a chain of events.

Have problems or defects that may be causing your property to linger for sale been discussed in this meeting? These issues made public can and certainly will be used against you. It has now been discussed in a group, in which everyone who wants to sell your property is working to do so as a buyer's agent. At what cost and in whose best interest and advantage are they working for? At this point it is certainly not the seller's.

Only one person present supposedly works for you. Your agent should refuse to publicly and in front of your adversaries (their office members) no less, to discuss anything that is sensitive and compromising in nature. The other 19 people present can use this information against you and for the advantage of their buyers' interests. But does the seller's agent refuse to publicly discuss your properties defects in the office meeting? How are you to know? The lines are very blurry and confused.

Seller's agents and buyer's agents do not belong in the same office together. They do not belong at the same sales meetings together. They should not share and be privy to the same information. They should not have equal access to so much sensitive information.

Attorneys do not share and openly mix interests. You cannot hire one unless a background check is made to insure that not only that particular attorney but any attorney in the entire firm, does not have a potential conflict of interest. Professional sports teams do not share the same playbooks and strategies with their opponents. They cannot even film the opposing team to gain unfair advantage. Elevators in hospitals have placards that stress the importance of discretion concerning patient information. These written warning signs inform medical professionals that confidential conversations should be avoided while in mixed company. Why, oh why, is your information, and therefore money, any less important to the real estate professionals of America? Because the system of representation has changed entirely but the way they all still do business has not changed in the slightest. They think about themselves first and the seller is an afterthought. They purport to have the seller's best interest covered but as I have pointed out in many different ways, the good of the seller is not even on their radar screen.

MULTIPLE LISTING SERVICE

Just about every sales entity utilizes the Multiple Listing Service (MLS): Realtors, agents, Internet sites, even their so-called competitors such as <u>Help U Sell</u> or <u>Assist 2 Sell</u>, will help sellers get on the MLS system. But are they doing you any favors?

Through the MLS, buyer's agents and therefore buyers have access to what should be treated as the seller's privileged information. The MLS system does not differentiate between seller's interest and buyer's interests. MLS reports to all agents in the same way. There is no division or protection of privileged information. Unfortunately, it is only the sellers who need to be protected and this is just not done. There is very little information about the buyers that could be statistically shared, which could be considered sensitive. Interestingly enough, the co-mingling of this information makes the realtors jobs much easier as well.

Let me prove this accusation with just 3 words.

DAYS ON MARKET

Any buyer's agent who is a realtor and a member of MLS can simply look up, through the MLS, the complete history of any property. With a stroke of a key, they can inform a potential buyer how long a property has been for sale. The Multiple Listing Service shows exactly how many days the property has been on the market. How is this in the seller's best interest?

Most sharp buyers and their agents are going to judge your price based on how long your property has been for sale. They will attempt to negotiate very hard with a seller who has had their property on the market for any length of time. In fact, the more days a property has been on the market the less money they will usually offer. Make no mistake about this one, almost all buyers will ask this question and they always get an answer. The sad or frustrating part of this equation is that your selling agent, the very person responsible for protecting you, is also the very entity providing this critical information to the buyers. It is being used against you, and your agent and your agent's listing service provide this privileged information to your money's enemy?

The Multiple Listing Service is a tool that favors and is in the best interest of the buyers and their agents.

The statistic days on market is a great tool for the sellers but need not be shared with the buyers to the detriment of the seller's interest.

ORIGINAL ASKING PRICE

Original asking price is another loaded cannon pointed directly at the seller. Your agent files paperwork with the Multiple Listing Service every time you make a price change. Again, most buyers will be privy to this information through the information sharing of the MLS system to the buyer's agents. Once again, this insider information shall be used against you during negotiations.

If the seller has come down in price repeatedly over a short period of time, it spells out a particular negotiating strategy. If the seller has held firm, but over a very lengthy time frame, it spells out yet a different negotiating strategy. If the seller has repeatedly come down in price over an extended period it shows another way to negotiate. There are many different pictures that are painted using this information. My point is that any information that does not pertain to the exact nature of the property should be treated as privileged information. It should not be readily available for the world to access and use against sellers at critical stages of negotiations. How is this in the seller's best interest?

I do not know of any information that is shared on demand that helps the seller gain a wholesale advantage over the buyers. Why are the seller's agents and the largest sales system of real estate allowed to give advantage away to the buyers? It simply defies all logic and responsibility.

Average Selling Price

The Multiple Listing Service also publishes the average selling price as compared to the asking price on an area-by-area basis.

Let's assume that the figure for your particular area is 93%. This means that the average seller received or was negotiated down by 7% off of their asking price.

This is yet again another harmful piece of information to the seller.

Any good Buyer's agent will suggest to their clients that when they make an offer to negotiate at least 7% off the asking price because they know (MLS HAS TOLD THEM SO) that this is the usual reduction in price for that particular area.

AVERAGE SELLING PRICE PER SQUARE FOOT

MLS publishes this statistic as well. It may not seem that harmful at first glance, but all properties do not have the same qualities and features. How might this average be used against sellers?

Can it be used to pigeonhole a luxury home when this is just an average foe average construction? No other mass statistic concerning building values lumps the square footage price into just one single category. Square footage values should be broken down into at least 4 classifications based on the quality and type of construction.

Once again, this is fine information and statistics for the Seller. It should not be made available to the buyer, so that it will only in turn be used against the seller.

Withheld Information

Interestingly, the Multiple Listing Service gives out all kinds of damaging information about the Seller's property but the very information that they should be freely sharing for the world to see is withheld. **The address.**

Realtors often times do not display or include the property address on www.Realtor.com for the public to see. There are quite a few properties for sale through the Multiple Listing Service that do not include the address of the property that is for sale. Is this in a seller's best interest if the property address is kept a secret? Not usually. It is most often in the Realtors best interest because this way any buyer interested in the property needs to contact the listing Agent for further details. Listing Realtors want to have prospective buyers call them directly. This way they can establish a relationship with both the seller and buyer on a particular piece of property. In doing so if the Realtor now has a sale work out they double their income. In the real estate industry this is known as getting both sides of the deal. This avoids a commission split with another agent and essentially doubles that Realtors commission. Again, entirely in the Realtors best interest and not the sellers.

What this now creates is another of the industry's great mysteries! The Dual Agent or what I have termed the **"Double Agent."**

A dual agent is a **"Double Agent"**, and like a spy in the movies a

"Double Agent" is never a good thing. They work both sides. Who are they loyal to? Who do they have a fiduciary relationship with? Whose best interest are they working for? Where money is concerned it is never possible to serve two masters at the same time. Now they have created a situation with 3 opposing sides. The Realtors interest now becomes the third interest involved, which creates an unethical predicament that the Realtors have fought long and hard to justify.

If you want to sell your property efficiently, it needs to be fully exposed to the entire market place. This is the complete opposite of keeping it's location a secret for the Realtor's selfish, self centered financial motives. You want to tell the world. "This property is For Sale" this is what the property consists of, how much it will cost and where it is located. Come and See!

Realtors will try to justify this selfish behavior by suggesting that sellers do not want to be bothered with drive by lookers or unqualified buyers

This is completely contrary to modern marketing of any higher priced product or service. Take a good look around at other products. Do you see any manufacturers hiding the products that they are trying to sell? In advertising products for sale most companies show a picture, describe the product and tell you exactly where you can see, touch, taste and smell the product.

Your property should be marketed and put out for the world to see, it's in your best interest. Not selfishly hidden away for the sake of your agent' pocketbook.

Commercial Real Estate sites can be an even worse offender of this hide and seek situation. A potential buyer usually needs to register just to view the site. Once a buyer is on the site, their viewing is constantly interrupted and harassed with offers to purchase upgrade memberships in order to view all the properties. Then just when a serious buyer starts to really get into searching, the site starts blocking views because an upgrade, which comes with a price, is now required in order to see the "premium Properties.'

My question is, as a commercial property owner how does it help you if a potential buyer or tenant needs to pay in order to see that your property is for sale or lease? Your concern should be that a buyer might cut their search short and concentrate on the properties they saw for free. Never looking at the whole marketplace because they found enough of a selection to fill their needs and yours was not included because it was located in the "premium section." Is the inconvenience and time consumption necessary in order for a potential Buyer to stop, register and pay chasing away any potential buyers? Millions of dollars are at stake and hide and seek is being played with your property. Is this in your best interest? I think not!

The www.FreeRealEstateOffice.com does not require registration to view properties. It does not require a buyer to pay for membership. Log in, look and find. Your information is out there for the entire world to see quickly, easily, open and notoriously.

Multiple Listing Service Forms

The following examples come from actual Multiple Listing Service and Association of Realtor forms.

Their own language demonstrates how truly conflicting this system actually is.

How are these synonymous with the realtors' claims of a fiduciary capacity and reasonability to the Seller?

SELLERS STATEMENT OF CONDITION

Also known as
Property Disclosure Statement

This is a form prepared by the Association of Realtors and given to you by your listing agent for you – the seller -- to fill out when you list your property. Some states require this form.

This form starts with the sentence: "*The seller authorizes the brokers or salespersons to provide the following information to prospective buyers.*"

The form ends with a phrase that states *"Seller hereby acknowledges that the information set forth above is true and accurate to the best of my knowledge. I further agree to defend and indemnify the brokers and any subagents for disclosure of any of the information contained herein.*"

"*Buyer/prospective buyer acknowledges receipt of seller's statement of property condition before purchase. Buyer acknowledges that broker has not verified the information herein and buyer has been advised to verify information independently.*"

What you just filled out and signed states that you know what you are doing and saying, please pass out this form and right or wrong you can and will be held accountable for all the information it contained. Oh, by the way, if there is any trouble, don't look to your agent for help. Just the opposite, you are to help them. You are to defend them. You have accepted full responsibility.

In the chapter on HISTORY OF THE PROBLEM, vicarious

liability was explained with an example given of the huge impact lawsuits had created. Real estate agents and offices want to distance themselves from any liability so badly that they now give sellers self-incriminating forms that can and will be used against you.

Unfortunately, the new conflict system leaves you standing alone to the point that your own agent has you fill out forms that are nothing less than lawsuits waiting to bite you in the behind, and this form is proof positive.

The new conflict system is nothing more than the entire real estate industry working very hard to avoid all liability.

This form is loaded, and I mean loaded, with explosives. Under the current conflict system, the only person in the transaction who is supposedly working in your best interest just gave you a form to fill out that gives you full responsibility for any and all answers. Not only this, but on top of that they want you to defend them. Right or wrong they want the seller to indemnify them! Once again, at all costs agents protect themselves.

Questions about hazardous waste, easements, flood plains and wetlands are on this form. An inexperienced property owner is going to attempt to provide potentially dangerous answers to the one person who is supposed to protect them! And then that ally is going to pass out this information. These potentially wrong answers made to a buyer can have serious implications. Who should know the pitfalls of this form, the agent or the seller?

Are they acting as professionals with a fiduciary responsibility by placing the seller in this precarious position? I think not!

You are paying a professional who places you into this situation!

Is this a system full of conflict? You bet it is!

I have personally known a Board of Health agent who was considering purchasing a lot upon which to build a new house. This Board of Health professional hadn't a clue if any wetlands existed on this parcel of land. I had to show this person that there were wetlands on the prospective property and these wetlands presented some very real issues.

This Property Disclosure Form contains questions about wetlands. Here was a professional who, for a living, actually judges and critiques the works of various professional engineers concerning wetlands and how they might impact septic and sewer systems; and this person was clueless. How can the average property owner be expected to know what a wetland is or isn't when professionals are not always sure.

The real estate community will try to justify this behavior by crying foul that some states require this form. This may be very well and good, but where are their lobbying efforts to change or prevent the usage of this form? You can bet that if the wording was slightly different and it was the realtors and agents who had to defend and indemnify the seller, and not the other way around, changes would have occurred long before this form ever went into use.

What does the average property owner know about floodplains? Someone can live on a particular parcel of land for 50 years and never experience a flood. Does that mean it is or isn't in a flood plain? I suppose the average seller would review their history and say yes.

I do know that it is common for civil engineers to design for one hundred (100) year storm events. It might have been the right or wrong fifty years (50) that the seller has experienced. Is their answer correct now? How can their agent let them answer these questions? But the questions remain on the form because the sellers have all the liability and the agents have none.

What does the average property owner know about hazardous waste? This is a very broad subject that seems like an enormous moving target. Most property owners are really not qualified to make such an assessment.

I am not an attorney nor do I pretend to be one

But in laymen's terms please allow me to dissect some of the other language on this Property Disclosure Form.

"Seller authorizes broker" – you have given permission to broker to provide this information to buyer. So the broker is covered.

"Based upon seller knowledge"-- The seller knows exactly what they are doing and saying. These are presented as facts made only by the seller. The broker is covered once again.

"True and accurate to the best of your knowledge" -- Is this a guarantee of the facts?

"Defend and indemnify the broker" -- don't sue the agents and if necessary the seller shall protect the agents. Broker is covered yet again.

"Broker has not verified the information"-- broker has no knowledge if the facts are correct or otherwise. Who is the realty professional in this relationship? Once again, the broker's posterior is covered and the seller's is not.

You are paying a real estate professional thousands of dollars! I believe for this money the agent should be carefully verifying all the pertinent property information for the seller. But this form states otherwise.

I find it very disconcerting that on another form known as a Consumer Relationship Disclosure form there is included the statement: *"Real Estate agents do not have a duty to perform home, lead paint or insect inspections nor do they perform septic system, wetlands or environmental evaluation."*

It is fine that they do not have to perform inspections. It cannot be expected of the realtors, but what is troubling about this statement is the double standard in which they disclose they are not experts, but a seller should fill out a Property Disclosure Statement and be held to a standard higher than the agents themselves.

Please take comfort and don't waste time worrying that you are not an expert and therefore do not know the various answers. The agents themselves are telling you that they are not experts either and are likewise not qualified to answer.

Most of the questions asked on this form can be answered by the inspection reports (Principal #2) that you have had performed before the property has been made available for sale. Your attorney (Principal #4) can answer still others if there are any remaining questions that you have not been able to find the answers to. There might even be some questions that you simply to not know the answers to and it is perfectly fine to say that you do not know.

If any missing information should become an issue do not spend a lot of time worrying, a potential buyer will be given a fair chance to seek out any answers that they are looking for.

Based upon this form alone, the property disclosure form, disregarding all the other conflict that I have pointed out in the book, should be reason enough for you to question why you would choose to be involved in the conflict system with a listing realtor. Why are you using a seller's agent when his or her own liability is more important than your liability? Why are you using seller's agents when their knowledge is not utilized on your behalf to verify potentially difficult or erroneous information required on this disclosure form. Perhaps these realtors simply do not possess the knowledge or experience necessary, but why put yourself (the seller) in the same or worse predicament?

This practice demonstrates that sellers have all the exposure. Sellers perform most of the work realty professionals should be accomplishing. Why do you need them? Replace them with you own efforts and save the thousands of wasted dollars paid to these realtors.

On a related form known as a "Disclaimer Regarding Service Providers" are contained several clauses that are basically stating that the realty company that is referring companies such as home inspection and the like *"has not conducted an investigation into the qualifications or financial status of any of these service providers."* This statement is a way for the listing real estate agent's company to shrug off any responsibility if their referral turns out to be disappointing and troublesome.

If the real estate company does not know about the qualifications of the party that they are referring, then why are they referring them to you in the first place?

Do you give out referrals to restaurants where you have never eaten?

Let's look at the combined effect of the last 3 forms.

First, the seller is providing and is responsible for more information than they should be. Secondly, the agent is not an expert and will not verify any potentially erroneous information provided innocently by the seller. Thirdly and finally, if an agent makes a referral for an expert and that expert turns out to be a clown, you cannot blame the agent for the bad referral. Don't you need to question just what the real estate industry is accomplishing for sellers?

www.FreeRealEstateOffice.com tries to avoid this by not placing you in compromising situations such as these. A listing and advertising section by all related professionals is included on the site. But more importantly any and all of these professionals can publicly be critiqued on the site. Opinions and ratings can now be viewed before you hire any needed discipline. Fees, customer service, attitude, ability, timeliness are just some of the insight a Seller can glean by review of this section. Best of all, these opinions are from other sellers and are based upon their first hand experience in dealing with these professionals. This will attempt to keep everyone honest.

Deposit Money Conflicts

On another particular State-Wide Multiple Listing Service's Exclusive Right To Sell Listing Agreement, there is a clause that states "*in the event that the Seller's Broker is made a party to the lawsuit by virtue of acting as escrow agent, the Seller's Broker shall be entitled to recover reasonable attorney's fees and costs, which fees and costs may be deducted from the escrowed funds, if the Seller is the prevailing party.*"

Wait a minute here. I have stated before that I am not an attorney nor do I pretend to be one, but how can any realtor defend this as being nothing short of being completely and absolutely in the realtors' best interest.

Review this phrase backwards. The seller is the prevailing party. The seller won. The seller must have been right in this instance because someone has made a binding legal judgment to that effect. This has most probably taken effect form a court a law.

Then why does it state that the seller needs to pay the seller's broker? The buyer must be at fault for the seller to have prevailed. Why doesn't the seller's broker collect from the buyer?

Another troubling phrase is that the seller's broker will take this money out of the seller's escrow money. No questions here about when the seller's broker will get paid because this states that the realtor can pay his or herself immediately.

The seller's realtor and the Multiple Listing Service have set up this completely one-sided agreement. In who's best interest is this clause?

It is common to find another clause in typical Multiple Listing Contracts that states: "*Broker and Seller(s) shall share equally in the liquidated damages.*"

Why? Has the realtor presented a ready, willing and able buyer? They have most probably not, if things are at the liquidated damages stage. The realtor was hired to sell the property for a fee upon completion of the transaction. To prevent this abuse most attorneys will include some language in the Purchase and Sale Contracts that in effect states something such as: "Realtor shall only be paid if, as and when the deed to the property is exchanged."

The realtor has not earned his or her commission if the buyer does not actually become the new Owner of Record.

Why do these realtors believe they should share equally (50%/50%) in the liquidated damages? If the commission agreement is 5%, then would not 5% (if at all) of the liquidated damages seem more equitable.

Let's assume, for example, that the deposit is $20,000. What these realtors have arranged for themselves with this clause is a $10,000.00 payment and they would still have another bite of the commission apple when the property is put back up for sale and sold. They don't want 5% of $20,000.00, which is only $1,000.00. It seems this is simply not enough and they feel entitled to more.

I do not believe, at this point in the transaction, that the realtor is entitled to any of the deposit money whatsoever. They still have a job to complete and should not be paid until they have completed it. This is just another deceptive way to take advantage of the seller.

Since when did the realtor become an equal partner with the seller?

AGENCY DISCLOSURE

There exists so much conflict of interest regarding just who represents whom that most states require agents to pass out and have proof of receipt by signing a form known as a Real Estate Agency Disclosure Notice. Add into this mix the various forms and efforts that realtors have put into print as an attempt to cover their backsides surrounding the Dual Agent **("Double Agent")** issue and this whole thing gets a bit confusing.

I have a State Real Estate Agency Disclosure Notice that has two interesting clauses. The first clause is "<u>you have the responsibility to protect your own interests</u>." The other clause contains a warning in big bold print on the same form stating that this notice "<u>IS NOT A CONTRACT</u>."

Wait just a minute! Realtors actually want you to sign this from. Can this form now or at some point in the future be used against you? Is it proof positive that you are or were clear about the confusing situation of dual agency? I believe that by signing this form you just might have affirmed that you are completely clear on this matter and the fact that at the most important stage of the transaction, the negotiation stage, your agent will completely change the dynamics of his or her relationship with you by becoming a facilitator. Strange it is not a contract, but it will most probably be used to spell out that you understood a very confusing contractual relationship that exists only in the real estate world. Do not feel bad if you actually do not understand this. Just be grateful you never signed one of these disclosure notices.

It is not a contract, but it sure can be considered legal notice.

The first warning on this non-contract is exactly why I require you in **PRINCIPAL #4** to hire an attorney. To whom do you think you should entrust your best interest to, a lawyer or a real estate agent?

THE COMMISSION MYSTERY

Most property sellers do not know exactly what happens to the commission money that they are spending! It has remained a mystery because most sellers simply assume that the commission is evenly split up between the agents and offices involved, but this not the case.

One office (listing) always has control, and they decide what they want offer for commission splits. The second office (buyers) does not even know what the actual total commission offering is, so how can they judge what is a fair split? If the commission the seller agrees to is 6%, the seller has no way of knowing if the listing agent is offering the buyer's agent a fair split or perhaps 2% or 2 1/2% instead of an even 3. The listing office displays on the MLS what they are offering for a split, but interestingly enough; MLS does not display the true and accurate total commission that is being paid.

This truly does have a significant impact on the seller and the seller should know or at least question the realtors involved in their transaction to make sure the right things are being done with their money and in the seller's best interest.

"*Broker is authorized to cooperate with other brokers, and divide with other brokers such compensation in any manner acceptable to Broker.*"

This clause found on some listing agreements gives the listing agent full authority to play any commission games that he or she may choose and it is a mystery to the seller whether they are fair about commission splits or not. Notice that it does not require broker to cooperate, it only authorizes cooperation. This allows the listing broker the ability to discriminate as to who is dealt with for other real estate agents and who is not.

If you sign a form containing this clause, you as the seller have given carte blanche to the listing realtor to play any sort of greed game they may desire.

"*Any manner acceptable to Broker*" What is acceptable to the Seller is what really matters here and a prudent seller would demand full and even cooperation and compensation with all agents that wish to sell the property.

There is all kinds of bad blood between agents in this industry because of a clause such as this one. I have seen and heard of all kinds of abuse that stems from this very kind of blanket authorization. The selling public does not hear of the turmoil created by commission games played by greedy listing agents because the realtors and the Multiple Listing Service insulate the public from its in house problems and fighting. They attempt to maintain their public image by keeping a cap on all the negative commission fighting

Your Commission Dollars
Have Always Been a Secret To You!

This is "**the commission mystery**". Most people simply do not know just where their commission payment goes. They assume things are split fairly and equitably between all parties involved, when in actuality many problems exist.

I was recently involved in a transaction where the listing realtor only offered the buyer's agent (mine) a 1% commission. This was legitimately done on the MLS system. My agent did not realize this poor excuse of a co-broker commission split until after we had negotiated the deal. At that point, the other realtor's attitude was "too damned bad for you." Do you think I will ever have anything to do with that office again? Do you think my agent will ever deal with that agent or office in the future? Had we noticed earlier in the transaction, we would have made an issue out of this unfair play. Perhaps even to the point of affecting the sale. This would not have been in the seller's best interest, but from other conversations with this realtor I surmise that he would not have cared in the least.

Are you wondering what this has to do with you selling your property?

That's my point exactly! You do not know if the realtor that you are contemplating hiring has or is capable of the same behavior

If this realtor, or the one you are perhaps contemplating hiring, has repeatedly, chronically and greedily offered uneven, unfair commission splits to the outside brokerage community, then it will not take long for that group to take notice. Once this has occurred, alienation will take place because other agents will know that if they deal with that person or office they will be screwed out of significant a portion of their income.

This creates a situation where it is not in any seller's best interest to list with the entire office in question. These unfair commission splits have shrunk the available buyers that will see your property in that particular market if you should list with an agent or office that commits such behavior.

How are you to know? This is part of the commission mystery that affects all sellers.

This leads to another mystery in the process.

What is your agent's actual commission share with their broker or real estate office and more importantly what expenses are they responsible for paying? Most sellers assume that the realty office pays for all the agent's expenses, but this is simply not the case. In fact, I believe that most offices and companies fall far short of what they should be providing for sales support. Many realtors need to supplement what is done for advertising. The seller needs to know what the realtor is personally capable of paying for in out of pocket expenses to achieve success in marketing the property.

It is commonplace for producing agents to receive a larger share of the commission split, but is that enough.

What are the out of pocket expenses to the agent and does this agent have the financial resources to pay for these items.

Not all offices pay for all the advertising.

Some offices will pay for most of the expenses, but any specialty advertising such as colored flyers, open houses, and aerial photography is out of the pocket of the agent. This can lead to big money in some instances.

Don't assume just because your agent works for a large nationally recognized chain or branded company, that it is any different.

These offices have their standard advertising offering to their agents that therefore it trickles down to you.

They will place print ads in certain papers and for certain periods of time and will do the same with the Internet advertising. They have their own Internet sites and will place Internet ads in several of the very large regional newspaper Internet sites where they have bulk advertising rates. They are hesitant to vary from these because it is more costly to them.

But if an agent wants to go to a more local newspaper site that is much more relevant and specific and actually a better place to advertise in, it is more expensive due to lack of quantity and therefore usually comes out of the agent's pocket.

So what is the split and what is each prepared to offer and pay for? This is a mystery that is not usually solved until after you have already committed to a listing contract.

Do not assume in bad times that the bigger companies can spend more money on your property and advertising.

The fact is they feel the financial crunch just like everyone. When things get tough and property takes longer to sell, where do you think they will tighten their budget? Their single largest budget expense is advertising and if this expense is reduced your agent needs to suck it up. Can they? Will they?

One of the giant national companies just doubled their agent's royalty fees. Times are tough so charge the agents more?

Why does this remain a mystery to you?

Whose money is being spent to achieve an efficient sale for the highest possible price for your property and where is it going to come from? This is totally in your best interest to know the answers.

With the www.FreeRealEstateOffice.com, you need not worry about commission games or clauses such as this one that welcomes abuse of your funds and other's agents. Commission offerings to a buyer's agent are plainly displayed for all to see. By showing your property the buyer's agent has accepted the terms of commission and they no longer need to worry about commission splits with hostile or aggressive offices. They are no longer concerned about when and if the commission checks will be cut and sent by other offices. There is no longer a commission split between offices. T he entire commission is paid directly to only one office. This system has removed one of the agents from the sale system. Listing agents cannot fight with buying agents because listing agents do not exist on www.FreeRealEstateOffice.com. Sellers now save that expense and pay the type of agent who performs for them in presenting a buyer. No more mystery and fighting. One agent is offered a 2%, 2 1/2% or 3% commission and that same agent or company is paid that amount at the time of closing.

PART II

The way to change

COMMISSION COMPARISONS

$300,000 property sale

Current "Conflict System"

6% commission: = $18,000

Sold with both listing and Buyer's realtor involved

Commission Savings of   -0-

www.FreeRealEstateOffice.com system

3% commission to buyer's agent only

$9,000 commission plus advertising expenses of approximately $77 a week

Total expenses for 3 months including commission = $10,000

Total expenses for 6 months including commission = $11,000

Commission Savings of $7,000 to $8,000

www.FreeRealEstateOffice.com System

-0- commission: direct sale to buyer, no Realtors involved
Total expenses for 3 months = $1,000
Total expenses for 6 months = $1,900

Commission Savings of $15,600 to $16,600

$600,000 property sale

Current "Conflict System"

5% commission: = $30,000

Sold with both listing and Buyer's Realtors involved

Commission Savings of   -0-

www.FreeRealEstateOffice.com system

2.5% commission to buyer's agent only
$15,000 commission plus advertising expenses of approximately $77 a week
Total expenses for 3 month including commissions = $16,000
Total expenses for 6 months including commission = $17,000

Commission Savings of $13,000 to $14,000

www.FreeRealEstateOffice.com System

-0- commission: direct sale to buyer, no Realtors involved
Total expenses for 3 months = $1,000
Total expenses for 6 months = $2,000

Commission Savings of $28,000 to $29,000

$1,200,000 property sale

Current "Conflict System"

5% commission: = $60,000
Sold with both listing and Buyer's realtor involved

Commission Savings of   -0-

www.FreeRealEstateOffice.com system
2.5% commission to buyer's agent only
$30,000 commission plus advertising expenses of approximately $77 a week
Total expenses for 3 months including commissions = $31,000
Total expenses for 6 months including commissions = $32,000

Commission Savings of $28,000 to $29,000

www.FreeRealEstateOffice.com System
-0- commission: direct sale to buyer, no Realtors involved   -0-

Total expenses for 3 months = $1,000
Total expenses for 6 months = $2,000

Commission Savings of $58,000 to $59,000

Anticipated Seller Expenses

Online and online newspaper advertising:
Two major newspapers, everyday per week average $22
Two major newspapers, open house print ads every third weekend

                                          Average $36

Misc. allowance: Examples Google upgrade, Craig's List
Repositioning, other local advertising $19
Real Estate Internet sites: Most Listings are Free   FREE

    Total Weekly Budget   **$77**

Fixed expenses:
    Signage: 2 for sale and 2 open house directional $100

        Home Inspections: average $300

            Total   **$400**

3 months anticipated budget $1400

6 months anticipated budget $2400

THE 12 PRINCIPLES
FOR SUCCESSFUL INTERNET
REAL ESTATE SELLING

12 Principles for Successful Internet Real Estate Selling

1. Be brave and set the price. The Seller always has.

2. Perform all inspections before marketing the property

3. Honestly represent the exact nature and condition of the property.

4. Hire an attorney. Do so early on in the sales process.

5. Get proof of insurance from everyone

6. Anything you say can and will be used against you. Excess talk can cost you money.

7. Cooperate with and pay buyer's brokers and buyer's agents.

8. You can sell directly to buyers without an agent

9. Online advertising is cheap!

10. Showings are easy

11. Be effective and follow up

12. Information concerning the property becomes the property of the property

The 12 Online Sales Principles from "Real Estate 3.0" are a guide to help you through the online sales process of selling direct to buyers and buyer's agents. Most of the information in these Principles can be used with the www.FreeRealEstateOffice.com sales system and I encourage you to make use of them.

Please do not become intimidated by the sales process. It is easier than you think. If you can sell something on Ebay you can certainly use this system with ease.

I realize you are not a real estate professional, but please, you need to give yourself more credit than you probably realize. Let me show you that if realtors and agents can do it, then with the right tools you can do it even better. You know more about your particular piece of real estate than anyone. Without realizing it you already perform most of the heavy work involved in the sales process. You certainly care more than anyone that your property gets sold efficiently. Your focus is so much more intense because it is aimed in only one direction.

I recently met with a broker on a particular transaction. This broker enjoyed bragging that he is also on the State Board of Regulation, inferring that he is a big shot with extensive knowledge, enough knowledge to be a 'State Regulator." In fact, on the back of his real estate business card, perhaps illegally, he has printed or stamped his official state title and address.

He gives out what I can only describe as some sort of a dual business card. On one side he is a real estate agent, and on the other side he is a state official. I believe this is done just to impress people that they should deal with him because as he is so important.

Well, I need to tell you the rest of the story!

The property we were discussing was a parcel of land. It became apparent to me early on, while looking at the plan of land, that this self impressed government official/real estate professional did not know what he was looking at on the plan. Finally he admitted to everyone present that he in fact is unable to read plans.

The plans that this self-proclaimed expert could not read were of his very own back yard! That's right; the land that he wanted to buy was behind his house so that he could increase his current lot size. I don't share this with you to belittle this man. Many people cannot read plans. I share this with you to reassure you that you do not need to "know it all" in order to sell your property. Here is a self-professed expert in real estate and real estate regulations and he literally is not able to find his back yard! He has survived for quite awhile making a living selling real estate and you too can survive selling you own real estate.

If you follow the 12 Principles from "Real Estate 3.0" as best that you can – not perfectly – the rest will fall into place and you will save thousands of dollars in unnecessary commission expenses and sell your property far more efficiently.

1. Be Brave and Set the Price
– The Seller Always Has

Don't be afraid! Most Sellers know exactly what their property is worth, especially the sellers of owner-occupied properties. Long before the Internet, most sellers were aware of what's going on around the area and what's been sold and for how much. Sellers usually know the area property history better than most realtors.

Now with the Internet, it is so easy to pull up your area and see where your property fits into the local marketplace. Sites such as www.googlebase.com, www.trulia.com and www.Realtor.com have everything most people need to use for comparable properties.

Be careful not to use automatic price values that are available on many of the Internet sites. Sites such Zillow publish what they refer to as a Zestimate of value but these values can range by a ridiculous amount of money, often ($200,000.) several hundred thousand dollars and more.

If you actually are unsure of where you property fits into the market, simply review the information on the Internet about what is for sale and what has recently sold in your particular area for similar properties. Where you fit into the local market is actually the key to the pricing process. Separate the other properties into two categories:

1) the properties that are just a little better than yours; and 2) the properties that are not quite as good as yours. Your property is in between these two groups and so should your price.

Yes there are exceptions to this and every rule but almost always a quick look at similar properties that are for sale and similar ones that have sold recently and it will be fairly easy to figure out the pricing.

If a seller it truly baffled on pricing, an appraiser can always be considered or consider paying a local real estate agent $100. to perform a current market analysis. Let them know that you are self-marketing and that you want to pay for their services. They will invariably try to talk you out of self-marketing but your honesty will go far and perhaps they will be back with the buyer you are looking for.

I have a friend with a house currently on the market. In this tough real estate market her agent is constantly on her back to reduce the price. I took one quick review of the local market where this property is located and I quickly assured her not to listen to her Realtor. Her home is priced exactly where it belongs. Not as high as the better houses and above the houses that are not as good. Any reduction in her price and she is simply competing with herself. Any buyer who wants a property of her caliber will surely see her house as well as the other similar properties that are for sale. It does not make any sense for her to adjust the price down below the competing houses when these other properties cannot compare. They are what they are and her property is better. Her property needs to be priced higher to reflect this. A little better property should have a price that is a little higher. A property that is much better, at a much higher price.

As a seller, please do not be afraid to price your property accurately. In some states Realtors are taking and entering listings into the Multiple Listing Service (MLS) with a high and low price such as $599,000 to $699,000. A One Hundred Thousand Dollar ($100,000.) price swing simply does not make any sense and is frightening to witness. In this market or in any market what buyer in their right mind is going to pay the high price? If a Realtor cannot properly appraise the value of a property, why would a seller consider doing business with that Realtor? Where is this Realtor's manager, and if there is so little oversight that they cannot or will not set a value, then why would you place your most valuable asset in their care? Why would the National Association of Realtors (NAR) allow such a self-destructive practice under their leadership? My point is that if these so called professionals are so wishy washy about price then you as a seller with complete familiarity with the property should have the fortitude to set a realistic price.

A common pricing mistake sellers do make is known as "Testing the Market." This poor practice has actually been performed by sellers and enabled by agents over the years for several reasons. It has traditionally been easy for a seller to persuade a realtor to take an overpriced listing. It is easy for the seller because the realtor is the one spending effort and money to move an overpriced property. The seller will come down to reasonable price after the seller has been satisfied that "they are not leaving anything on the table." And the seller will still keep the listing with that same realtor when they lower the price of the property. After all, the seller has everything to gain and nothing to loose.

Wrong!

What has just happened in this common scenario? If this "Testing of the Market" by adding fluff to the price sounds familiar to you, then I have just made my point. You (the seller) have just set the price. You always have! The seller sets the price by pushing it up higher and the realtor agrees and lets the seller do it.

Let me paint the picture of how a typical market analysis takes place.

A seller considering placing their property on the market will typically call two to three local agents to perform a market analysis. The real estate community likes to call them a Current Market Analysis (CMA). All three agents will come over and see the property and all three agents will usually come back with differing figures. The particular agent that the sellers happen to like, based on personality, experience and energy (great traits in a salesperson) does not have the highest estimate of value. In fact, the sellers disagree with all three current market analysis and on top of that, the sellers want to test the market!

Let's look at this even further. The next step will usually be that the sellers express their disappointment to their favorite candidate because they feel all the CMA's are too low in price. In fact, this agent was the lowest in estimate of value but the sellers want to go with this agent because they like this agent. What happens next is that agent will almost always agree to take the overpriced listing at the seller's desired price and try it out "for awhile." He or she might even agree to follow the seller's desire and test the market even further by going up even higher in the original pricing.

Notice that the seller set the price by pushing it up higher than all the estimates of value and the realtor agreed and let the seller do so.

So what's the harm in this? Plenty!

Properties that are priced accurately sell quicker and for a greater amount of the asking price.

If the property stays on the market for any length of time it will cost the seller real money.

Every day you own and carry your property, it costs you money that you will never get back. I have never seen a transaction in which the sale price was added to the carrying costs that were accumulated while the property was for sale and then added together for a new price that was adjusted higher at the closing.

Daily, taxes, insurance, mortgage principle and interest are adding up.

As an example, let's say your home is worth $300,000 and you place this property on the market for $375,000 to "test the market." After 8 months and 3 listing price reductions later and it finally sells for the $300,000 that it was always worth.

The figures breakdown like this;
$300,000 Sales price
- 9,600 minus 8 mortgage payments (consisting of almost all interest)
- 4,666 minus 8 months of real estate taxes ($7000/year)
- <u>400</u> minus 8 months of insurance ($600/year)
$285,334 Net amount after expenses

$300,000. Sale price
  285,334 net amount after 8 months expenses

$14,666.

It costs almost $15,000 to test the market.

Now let's look at an efficient sale.

You price the property at $304,900 and accept the same $300,000 as above only this time it sells in 1 month because it was priced accurately.

$300,000 Sale Price
-    1,200 minus 1 mortgage payment
-     583 minus 1 months real estate taxes
-     <u>   50</u> minus 1 month's insurance

$298,167

It costs $1,833 to sell in one month.

Compare the two different scenarios with the only difference bring that of time. Both accepted the same $300,000.

$285,334. Net after marketing for 8 months or

<u>$298,167.</u> Net in one just month

$12,833.   INCREASE IN MONEY TO THE SELLER BY SELLING THE PROPERTY MORE EFFIECENTLY AND IN LESS TIME

This is a savings of almost thirteen thousand dollars, simply by not testing the market and selling the property more efficiently. Seven months time and $13,000 more in your pocket by not playing the all too tempting "test the market" game!

Another problem with "testing the market," is that you chase away the initial and largest pool of buyers. Many serious buyers are monitoring the market, your market, this very minute. They have seen all there is for sale in a certain price range and in a certain target location and have not yet found anything that they want or like. They wait and watch and when something new comes on the market, it shows up on their radar screen and they have instant interest in the newcomer. If your property is too high, they will by-pass it knowing it is too high or they will bypass it because of the combination of these reasons. The price is too high and since you just put it on the market you will most probably not be ready or realistic enough to negotiate very much. The buyer's attitude will be that it is too soon for seller to get real.

Yet another reason not to play the "test the market" game is that in tough times or in a down market when property values are declining your property could actually be worth less in 10 or 11 months than it currently is. Time equals money and the test period can create a loss situation.

So I have shown you that testing the market it can potentially cost you money and now I have highlighted the fact that testing the market can cost you opportunity as well.

But don't be afraid. My point to all of this is that you most probably know what your property is worth and that you always have. Do not be shy and second-guess yourself. I will bet that if you spent one hour on a used car lot you could figure out what your car is worth. Spend a few hours and you will be surprised how easy it is to come up with the value of your real property. Now I want you to set your own price and stop with the test games.

You know what your property it is worth, so price it accordingly and then efficiently sell it.

You as the owner, especially if owner occupied property, have such an advantage of knowing your market – use it to your benefit.

If you truly are struggling with setting a price, we have included a program on our site www.FreeRealEstateOffice.com that will establish a value for you, as well as a map of area comparable properties for you to analyze. Simply review these on our Website. But I must caution you. Again, you have knowledge about the local market and you know the value of your real estate. Stick to your guns and put this knowledge to good use.

2. You Must Perform All Inspections Before You Market the Property.

This is done for several very important reasons.

The first reason is that in order to price your property accurately, you need to know the exact condition of your property. Very few people are construction experts who can, for example, judge the condition and remaining life expectancy of a roof. As the owner you are aware of information pertaining to the roof such as age and perhaps that it has never leaked. But you need to know the exact condition of the roof in order to avoid future problems in the sales transaction. A professional report gives you the exact condition of the entire structure including the roof. As a seller, you are now conveying the condition of the property based on a professional's opinion. A professional who also carries error and omissions insurance, which guarantees your protection against claims if the professional, and not the seller, is incorrect about the condition.

I am not suggesting that you need to perform any repairs that are highlighted in the report. In the above example of the roof a seller can now inform a buyer with all confidence that "according to the inspection report the roof is in fine condition," or perhaps "according to the inspection report the roof needs replacement." But, this has already been taken into account and is reflected in the asking price. You see, as a seller, there were no surprises after the negotiations that cost you money.

The second reason you need to do this is one of my pet peeves with listing (sellers) agents. It is beyond me why they do not suggest this money saving idea to their sellers.

Inspections performed and used by the seller before a sale is made will avoid a renegotiation of the sale price after the agreement of sale. These renegotiations are always, always, always downward of the initial agreed to sales price. These renegotiations come out of the seller's pocket. Buyers never perform an inspection after the sales agreement and come back to the seller saying that things are in much better shape than they expected, so here is an extra $10,000.

Just the opposite will occur. Inspections, performed by the buyer after a price agreement, present the perfect opportunity for the buyers and their agents to complain and drive the purchase price down through a second round of negotiations.

Listing agents should know better than to let their sellers fall into this negotiation trap, but they don't. Didn't you hire them because they can negotiate on your behalf? This is proof once again that they do not negotiate on the seller's behalf and that you do not need a listing realtor.

I also feel it is particularly poor timing now that everyone has become familiar with the seller and the sellers negotiating style, or reasons or temperament, from the first round of negotiations, to attempt another bite of the price apple through the use of the inspection reports.

Take this ability to renegotiate away by performing the inspections yourself, before a buyer is found and a sale is made. You need these inspection reports anyway in order to price the exact condition of your property. So why not have them done at a small expense and use them to your advantage, potentially saving thousands of dollars.

Inspections only cost a few hundred dollars. This is many times less than what it could or would cost you in renegotiations. Have the inspections performed before you put the property on the market and avoid any surprises. Use the reports to gain and assemble the exact nature of your property so you can price the property fairly, blemishes and all.

Have your inspection companies email your reports to you at your property filing cabinet address at the www.FreeRealEstateOffice.com. Then prior to a buyer making an offer to purchase your property, the buyer must acknowledge that these reports were shared and received by them. The reports will be located automatically in the property filing cabinet of your sales office, so sharing them will be simple and automatic.

Your buyers may ask to have their own inspection performed even though you have already done so as I suggested. This is perfectly acceptable for them to request and you should let them. This second inspection also needs to be emailed to the property filing cabinet, just like the one the seller had performed earlier; and by prior agreement, it becomes part of the seller's records as well. If this second report comes up with anything that your inspector had missed or overlooked, then it will be up to your inspector or the inspection companies insurance to make good for the oversight. Again you have been insulated from receiving a lesser price.

Remember, anyone and I mean anyone, working for you including your home inspector, will need to give you proof of satisfactory error and omissions insurance before they are hired and paid. Do not make any exceptions.

You perform all the needed inspections in advance to save money and aggravation. This way you avoid a price renegotiation. You have already gone through one negotiation, and there is absolutely no reason to go through another one.

Remember to share this data before any offers. Accept no offers until buyers have received this information. This way everyone is up to speed and on the same "present conditions" page.

3. Honestly Represent the Exact Nature and Condition of the Property.

Honesty is always the best policy and concerning real property it is also the least expensive. Dishonesty can cost a seller a fortune in legal fees and damages. Do not misrepresent the property condition. Do not commit this crime.

The www.FreeRealEstateOffice.com sales system is set up to keep the seller as protected from trouble as possible. Every professional you hire has to provide you with proof of insurance coverage. This means the only person who should be cautioned about misleading a buyer is the seller. In order to avoid any misunderstanding, you need to disclose the exact nature of your property.

However, you do not and should not disclose the nature about yourself, only the property.

If you've had water in the basement, clearly state when, where and how much water you have had. Don't be shy. Someone will still want to own the property just as you did.

Make sure this or any disclosure made by the Seller is documented somewhere, on the inspection report, the property information report or on the purchase agreement. Your attorney can do this for you. Don't be concerned about this process. It's not that difficult; and I want you to avoid any trouble and have a clean sale.

Remember that a prudent buyer needs all the facts to make a sound decision to purchase. You must give them all facts that could affect their decision making process.

If you do not know an answer to a question, the best answer is just that---"you simply do not know."

For example, if you were asked where your rear lot line is? I do not know is a perfectly acceptable and safe answer. If you do not know say so. Never guess. You are most probably not an engineer or surveyor (don't be frightened, neither are the buyers.) The buyers will be given the chance to hire an engineer if they so desire one to clarify the point.

How old is the roof?

What does your inspection say – share this fact, from the inspection report, with the Buyer?

Where is or how good is the septic system working? Again, what does it say on your inspection report.

How is the furnace?

Again, rely on your inspection report. What does it say? Share it with the buyer.

If you know for a fact some information that should be shared, positive or negative, you need to disclose such information.

On the other hand if you do not know the answer to a given question do not guess at the answer. Simply state that you do not know. It's okay --- in fact it is better not to know the answer as long as you state so as your response. You do not have to be a real estate expert. So do not pretend to be one. It is perfectly acceptable not to know the answer.

Rely on your inspectors to know most of the answers and share these reports for your own protection.

Use your attorney to clarify any information concerning what to share and document. Your attorney is 100% on your side and this is why you have hired him or her. Use his or her experience; it's only a call, or better yet, an email away.

I need to caution all sellers here. Just as it is critically important to disclose what is important for information pertaining to the property, it is just as important not to disclose personal information (**Principal #6**) about you and your life.

The exact nature of the property has nothing to do with the exact nature of your life. Keep this distinct information separate and completely to yourself. It has absolutely no bearing on the property and can only be used against you.

4. Hire an Attorney.
Do So Early on in the Sales Process.

Attorneys as a whole get a bad rap. We have all heard the jokes, but I believe attorneys are completely necessary in a real estate transaction in order to protect the seller's best interest. Unlike a divorce or lawsuit, selling your real property should not be an adversarial process. You want to sell and someone wants to buy, so this objective (with differing interests) needs to be accomplished. There should be no reason to fight. Negotiate, yes. Fight, no. Good legal counsel will facilitate the sales process.

In order to complete the sale, the seller will need to have a deed prepared to convey the property to the new owners. Many sellers turn to an attorney to prepare the deed. A deed is a very simple instrument to prepare. Most often, it is as easy as changing a few pertinent facts. If you attempt to hire an attorney to only perform the work of a deed preparation, they will generally charge much more than the work costs and rightfully so. A deed costs less than $50 to prepare and a seller can be charged anywhere from $300 to $600 for the work. Besides the small expense in labor and time incurred preparing the new deed, an attorney also needs be concerned with any future issues that could arise and charge for the unforeseen problems and liability. Please do not feel that I am defending this, but this action does make business sense. My point is that it is actually very short money to hire this same attorney to represent you for the entire transaction. It should cost a total of around $700 to $1,000 for a basic real estate transaction. It only makes complete financial and common sense to have legal coverage for the difference of between $200 to $500 dollars.

Every party in a real estate transaction generally has legal representation.

The bank will definitely have an attorney, the buyer will usually hire an attorney and title insurance companies will hire an attorney. Why not the seller? Spend the money. Think of it as protection, guidance and insurance. You'll spend $1,000 to insure $20,000 car. Why not spend that same $1,000 to insure a smooth $200,000 or $2,000,000 property sale. Another caution I must make is not to share an attorney with any of these other groups. Take for example the common practice of sharing the banks' lawyer to save a few bucks. If there is ever a problem this attorney will always chose the side of his or her original client and you will be left out in the cold. Sellers need their own legal protection and representation.

Your transfer of property requires contracts. Unless you are an expert, don't pretend to be one. One sentence added or deleted in a contract can change it entirely. Don't risk it. Have your attorney review any and all documents **before** you sign them.

In some areas of the country the use of attorneys in real estate transactions is prolific. In other areas title companies are used and in other areas they make use of escrow companies to complete the transfer of ownership. Consider that escrow and title firms facilitate the process and do not work entirely in the seller's best interest. It is short money to get complete protection of your own council. Commit to hire legal counsel early on, up front.

Negotiating Table

One of the great features on www.FreeRealEstateOffice.com system is the custom negotiators office. This office is accessible to a potential buyer only when they become a real buyer and seek to negotiate an offer on your property. The negotiators section has several different types of offers that a buyer can fill out and send to the seller. All of this is performed online at the conference table so that the sellers can take full advantage of the built in feature that prevents the buyer or buyer's agent from negotiating live, face to face, or live over the phone. Negotiation should be done using the online forms and system. But if the negotiation should require more of a meeting of the minds, this is a great time to involve your lawyer. Your attorney can talk live to the buyer's side if need be, but you as the seller should be cautious of live negotiations.

Once you have agreed to the basic terms of sale with the buyer, you will need to have a more formal and lengthy contract known as "The Purchase and Sales Agreement" prepared and executed. A sample Purchase and Sales Agreement can be found at the end of this section or on www.FreeRealEstateOffice.com. Keep in mind that the inclusion of differing clauses from state to state keeps this document from being a one size fits all, boilerplate type of an agreement. Because of this fact, included on the site are companies that specialize and sell these agreements on a state-by-state basis. And if you paid attention to **Principle #4** your attorney is actually the best place to have this agreement drafted.

Once this agreement has been prepared it should be emailed into your property filing cabinet so that everyone involved in the transaction will be able to evaluate, modify and execute the contract when there is final agreement.

Several of the other great benefits to this virtual contract system is that the many parties involved in the transaction shall be automatically updated and copied from this point on, right down to scheduling the closing. Now everyone in need of the sales information can be copied and updated automatically. It will no longer be necessary to place ten phone calls because you are wondering where your contracts are and who is holding things up. The hold-up party in the process now becomes transparent and obvious for all to see, which will effectively produce more efficiency.

PROFESSIONALS RATING PAGE

I have worked with hundreds of real estate attorneys and with the exception of maybe two they have all been professional, knowledgeable and extremely helpful.

Providing safe, careful, thoughtful and competent advice to complete the desired outcome (selling) while guiding a client properly through the process is the service they provide.

Good legal counsel will enable the sales process.

Bad legal advice will stifle the sales transaction.

A "deal killer" is an attorney who decides to completely change the entire transaction even to the counter desires of the seller. This in turn ruins the sale. I don't know why, maybe it's an ego thing, but these types do exist. Fortunately these types few and far between. I have only come across this type of an attorney twice and I can remember them both as if it were yesterday.

As a safety for this kind of behavior from all the professionals involved in the transaction, there is a built in section on the website where sellers can comment and rate any of theses professionals: attorneys, inspectors, inspection companies, buyer's agents, title companies, escrow agents and appraisers -- any service provider.

This system will allow you to see how other sellers have felt, what they have paid for services or how they have been treated. Did they receive everything that they were promised or sold? This rating service is available for any seller on www.FreeRealEstateOffice.com to utilize as a resource before and after hiring decisions have been made.

This is a very unique component of our system. Please add and contribute to it. The benefits to everyone will be enormous.

One last item regarding the use of an attorney, **Principal #6** states that anything you say can and will be used against you. If you are stuck for an answer concerning your property, seek your lawyer's counsel to provide the correct answer.

5. Proof of Insurance from Everyone

The real reason the Real Estate Industry changed the original format to the current "**conflict filled system**" was because of the lawsuits and large judgments being awarded to wronged or injured parties. These lawsuits were costing the realtors, insurance companies and sellers a fortune. The Realtors and insurance companies changed the system to save themselves from the lawsuit judgments. Notice once again these changes didn't necessarily save the sellers any money.

Regardless of who was at fault, sellers blamed agents, agents blamed sellers, and buyers blamed everyone. The bottom line is that everyone but the Seller had and still is required to have insurance coverage.

Pressure by so many insurance companies was actually one of the main catalysts for the changes in the real estate industry.

Quite simply, the insurance companies were paying out far too much in damages. Then the insurance companies started hitting the agents very hard by refusing to write error and omissions insurance or by charging outrageous premiums for the error and omissions policies. This push back eventually became one of the reasons that the real estate industry changed to the current conflict-filled system.

So now that I have explained to you that insurance issues were so enormous that insurance companies were one of the root causes for the change in seller representation, you must by now understand that the issue of insurance is critical in the real estate sales process. Now, let me ask you a question!

Do you have any knowledge as to what kind of insurance your past or present real estate agents have or ever had? Who is or was their insurance company? How much error and omissions insurance coverage do they have? Have they actually paid their premiums and is the insurance coverage even in effect?

Sellers need to follow the lead of the insurance companies!

It is time we turned the tables to protect the sellers with the very same information and requirements.

Do you realize that builders and developers must prove to their own insurance, not other companies but too their own insurance company, that everyone, every subcontractor, general contractor, supplier, everyone that works directly or indirectly for them has insurance coverage of their own?

This is done to protect their insurance company. Not to protect the developer or builder. If there is a problem, the builder's insurance company wants proof from the builder that everyone else working for them has their own insurance. This way the builder's insurance company will not need to pay for any claims. The insurance companies are so serious about this that once a year they send and auditor to look at the builder's records to make sure that this requirement for proof of insurance is followed to the letter and with no forgiveness.

So, sellers we are now going to handle things the same way. We are going to learn and follow the insurance companies' lead.

Everyone, every professional working for you or working for the buyer, that comes into contact with your property MUST submit proof of insurance to the seller.

The reasoning is quite the same as the insurance companies that started this procedure. This protects the seller from any claims. If any professional involved in the transaction should make an error or an omission the seller can rest assured that there is an insurance policy behind that individual or professional. If at a future date a problem is discovered, the insurance information survives on in the property filing cabinet. Not all professionals have the capability to make good financially for a mistake, so it is highly important that they have proper insurance.

Everyone, every professional working for you or working for the buyer, that comes into contact with your property MUST submit proof of insurance to the Seller. This is without exception. I mean everyone! Your attorney, inspectors, engineers and consultants all need to provide a certificate of insurance. Right down to the company that owns the septic tank clean-out truck. Buyer's agents and any companies or professionals that have reason to enter upon the property need to provide proof of proper insurance coverage as well.

One of the benefits to buyer agency is that buyer and buyer's agent conflicts are insulated from the seller. What takes place between them should stay between them, but just to make sure there is no overflow of problems onto the seller, we require proof that buyer's agents have proof of insurance coverage.

This is an easy process and is performed online. The website will instruct anyone you have hired, as well as all buyer's agents, who wants to show your property (before they show it), how they or their insurance company can submit the required information to your property filing cabinet.

Now you are covered by other parties' insurance for other parties' potential problems or mistakes. This is exactly as it should be.

6. Anything You Say Can and Will be Used Against You!

I don't necessarily mean in a Court of Law. I mean in your bank account! Personal information can cost you money. Savvy buyers and their agents will use your personal information and stories to find a way to pay you less money for you property.

You need to understand that in the world of negotiations, information is power, and I do not want you to make the mistake of giving the other side any advantage over you.

The buyers may seem to be exactly like the kind of people you desire to carry on and care for the property where you have so many fond memorizes. Please do not let these emotions cloud the fact that this is a business transaction. The buyers want your property and for the least amount of money as possible.

You need to stick to the facts concerning the exact nature of your property and not your exact nature or your life. Unless you are a celebrity they are not purchasing your real estate for you or your memories.

In fact, the more you remain a mystery the better. Keep as much of your personality removed from the transaction as possible. Be a cordial host and be a good listener. Answer any and all questions that pertain to the property.

Some examples of how personal stories can harm your pocketbook go something like this:

You share with the buyers the fact that your knees are very bad and you need to have surgery performed on them. All the while you are standing in the home, you are trying desperately to sell what just so happens to be a multi-level home that has stairs absolutely everywhere. Don't you think a light might go off in the buyer's negotiating brain that says Ah Ha this person really needs, not necessarily wants, to sell this home for critical health reasons? At offer time maybe they will test just how critical it is for this seller to sell.

Perhaps you share that you are in the midst of a grueling divorce and yes, once again the buyers think Ah Ha lets find out just how badly this seller needs to get out and get away from this present situation.

Or maybe your husband says something casual, for instance, how he is getting sick and tired of being here for the last 30 Sunday afternoons for open houses.

Again the buyer thinks: Ah Ha this guy has been trying to sell for so long that he is sick of the process. Maybe they will take less to end the situation.

And this list goes on and on. So you see keep conversation light and be a good host. Make them feel comfortable, but narrow what you say down to harmless pleasantries and just the facts about the property – NOT YOUR LIFE   STORY.

When asked the inevitable and all encompassing question, why are you selling? Keep the answer very simple. All you need to respond with is something like; "it is a good time in your life to sell" or "it is now good timing for you to make a change."

One of the big problems with the current "conflict system" of real estate sales is that all the wrong people have way too much access to your information and it is freely shared with everyone and their brother. Don't be as guilty of sharing harmful information with the buyers as most of the real estate community has been.

This system is designed to eliminate this co-mingling of information, if you will just follow some simple guidelines.

Showings and appointments can and should be scheduled on line if possible.

Your face-to-face meetings with buyers or agents should be limited to a showing or two. Besides pleasantries, any conversations should be limited to the exact nature of the property. Answer only questions about your property.

All other communication between seller and buyers and buyer's agents will take place online at the conference table on the property Website.

Most importantly, all offers shall be submitted to the negotiations office online. Not presented over the phone by an agent and never presented in person by an agent or the buyer. Agents are instructed and cautioned that in order to remain in good standing they must abide by this principle. Additional negotiations can and will take place with your permission through your attorney. Additional requests for information need to take place online as well.

On the flip side, be a good listener and perhaps you will learn things you can use to get the upper hand. Maybe the potential buyer has been transferred and is living out of a motel from Monday to Thursday for the last 24 weeks and without his or her family. This would tell you that if they like your property, it should be a no-nonsense transaction and now you can strive to keep it just that way.

Please remember, unless it is said in private to one of your employees (attorney, inspector, consultants), your personal information can and will be used against you and it will usually cost you money.

7. Cooperate With and Pay Buyer's Brokers

Your primary mission is to sell your property. To do so effectively, you must expose your property to the entire marketplace. Buyers agents have exactly what you need – buyers. They represent the largest single pool of buyers in the entire marketplace. It makes absolutely no sense to exclude them from this process. Why in the world would anyone choose to dismiss this position and their viability? Embrace the position of buyer's agents in the process and gladly pay them. Their commission expense represents a cost of doing efficient business and is completely necessary and reasonable.

I preach that you do not need to waste your money on selling or listing agents. Please do not confuse this with buyer's agents. If an agent brings you a buyer be more than gracious and pay them for their efforts.

The www.FreeRealEstateOffice.com system requires that a commission offering be posted for the buyer's agents. This will avoid all the trouble that takes place in the current conflict system because now the involvement by agents is singular, only one agent or realtor per sale, so there are no other agents to fight with over commission splits and payment or even the ownership of customers. Agents shall also know exactly how much compensation they shall receive before they decide to cooperate with a seller and show their property.

When you place any advertising, make sure that you include

the phrase "brokers protected" or "agents welcome" in your ad. By including this phase buyer's agents will know that you are prepared to cooperate and pay them if they secure a purchaser for your property.

This system is not traditional "For Sale by Owner" also known by the acronym FSBO. This system is Real Estate 3.0. Ushering in a new era in how real estate is sold. Offering Sellers a new method to complete their entire real estate transactions over the Internet.

Placing your property for sale by owner (FSBO) is a completely foolish mistake.

Real Estate 3.0 not only welcomes cooperation between sellers and buyer's agents, we have also established an entire system that far exceeds anything created to date, that fully enhances and fosters many forms of contact and communication between sellers, buyers and buyer's agents.

Most for sale by owner handle things just the opposite of the www.FreeRealEstateOffice.com system. FSBO's are generally a very individualistic type who can and will do things on his or her own. They do not wish to be bothered by the real estate brokerage community and want to be left completely alone.

Combine this with the new "Do Not Call Lists" that have been initiated in most states and FSBO's have become a foolish group that has left themselves unapproachable by most agents.

The Do Not Call List makes it illegal for sales companies to contact and solicit people at their homes if they are on the list. Real estate agents are understandably hesitant to approach a FSBO about their property even though the agent knows he or she has the perfect match of both property features and buyer. They will not, must not, approach For Sale By Owner's! They are cautioned all the time by office management not to disobey this law and risk a fine to themselves and the company.

Do you think that agents will inform buyers about FSBO properties that they certainly will not be paid for? The odds are against it!

So, by attempting to sell as a FSBO, you have completely alienated an enormous segment of the marketplace. This is not so with Real Estate 3.0.

The www.FreeRealEstateOffice.com system enables and encourages you to sell directly to a buyer if they are not working with an agent. But if they are working through an agent, in order to utilize our system and services you must commit, up front, to cooperate and pay a commission to the buyer's agent.

8. You Can Sell Directly to Buyers Without an agent

The entire Sellers Listing System has been created around the central theme of seller attracting buyer and consummating the transaction online. The system takes the mystery out of the sales process and provides all the tools necessary for a seller to sell directly to a buyer. If a seller uses these built in tools and follows these 12 principals and hires the professionals suggested, then direct transactions are easily accomplished.

It is in your best interest to make as much as you can on the sale of your property. This system supports what is in your best interest.

The www.FreeRealEstateOffice.com has been arranged for the easy free flow and exchange of information accessible by anyone/anywhere.

We welcome buyers by providing them with direct easy access to the property information. There are no annoying squeeze pages and required registration needed in order to view the properties. Full property locations are listed on the property information pages. Full contact information linking buyers directly to the seller is listed online and on all signage.

At the sellers choice, contact can be made at one of several phone locations, email or posted online.

Before you have a direct showing with an interested purchaser, an initial showing that does not have an agent involved, simply make sure that the buyer electronically accepts the box confirming that an agent did not introduce them to your property.

This will prevent any future misunderstandings and avoid any unfounded commission claims.

It is that easy. Go forth and sell your property.

9. Internet Advertising is Cheap!

You need to get the fact that your home is for sale out there for the world to see.

In order for your property to sell in a reasonable amount of time (which in normal conditions should be six months or less) it needs to be priced property and fully exposed to the entire marketplace. Fortunately, you can easily control both of these variables.

With the enormous number of buyers using the Internet to search for property, it only makes perfect sense that you to use the Internet as your mainstay for marketing.

A three months online advertisement in the Los Angeles Times is only $99.00. That's $1.10 per day. It just doesn't get any better than this.

If you live near Los Angeles and wanted to sell a property, a good marketing plan would be place online newspaper ads in the Los Angeles Times and two other relevant newspapers. For the other two newspapers, I would choose a more local paper and then a community paper to cover small, medium and large markets or think of the coverage as neighborhood, area and regional.

If you need help in searching for area online newspapers in your area and how to contact them a good place to look is www.newspapers.com.

At these rates you could get superior online coverage in three publications for six months and it should cost you less than $600. Compare that to a 3% commission!

Print advertising is still very expensive and because of this I would limit print advertising to small line ads placed in Fridays' papers announcing your upcoming open house that weekend and perhaps small line ads in local papers that do not have an online audience but still generate some local action.

Get your information out there and online. Keeping your property a secret will not help sell it! For open houses, put the address in, along with a short description, price, phone number and the phrase "brokers welcome." If putting the address in the paper bothers you, at least consider including the neighborhood, village or area of town where the property is located. It is not uncommon for a buyer to have a pent-up need for a particular area (ex; school district) and they will respond rather quickly if it fits their criteria.

A common tactic that Realtors often utilize in their advertising and on www.realtor.com is to withhold locations and addresses. This is done as a way to force buyers to contact them directly. This practice of hide and seek with the address is in no shape or form helpful to sellers as they try to sell their property. This address mystery game is designed only to benefit the listing agent. It creates a situation in which the seller's agents will double her or his commission by becoming a DUAL or "**DOUBLE AGENT**." It's about the realtor's pocket and not yours when this information is withheld.

If you really want to sell, get the information out there.

Every property is unique and needs exposure.

The way most real estate offices advertise is by putting properties into categories. They use an example or two in each price grouping. A few properties from the lesser, medium and luxury categories are advertised to cover the market range. Maybe it's not your house that's in the advertisement but buyers can see the office has houses for sale in that price range. This is generally the reasoning behind this format.

Another piece of information that is not well known to the public is that if a listing realtor wants any advertising that is considered out of the norm, most real estate offices require that agent to pay for that advertising out of their own pocket. What if you have a great agent that who has a brilliant marketing idea for your property but personally money happens to be very tight for the agent and he or she cannot afford the extra expense? Does your marketing suffer because of this?

There is another issue that I have with the way larger offices place their online advertising. They often times limit the online advertising to newspapers where they get deals on bulk advertising rates.

Advertising in publications with the lowest cost is not always the most effective, and, the difference in cost is very short money. But, corporate decision-making will not allow the change to another online newspaper even though it makes perfect marketing sense.

Maybe it's fine if your market is truly drawn from the Wall Street Journal, but if not then an advertisement in this publication is done only to impress you and not to effectively market your property!

The issue with this is not that they use the Wall Street Journal, but typically, they will not place your ad online in a better market specific paper for your property because they do not have corporate bulk rate agreements with these other online newspapers; thereby missing publications your from which market is drawn.

If you have had the previous experience of selling a property through a listing agent, do you recall if the agent had ever given you a week-by-week breakdown or explanation of when and where your property was advertised?

I can tell you I have requested exactly this numerous times from several different agents and I have never once received such a breakdown. When I went to list the properties, the agents typically whipped out sorts of publications that they proudly advertise in, but never once after listing the property has any agent ever kept me informed, updated and copied on my property specific advertising.

I don't want to belabor the situation that many realtors and agents are completely ineffective at following up. Rather, I have attempted to bring you some awareness in the hope that you will gain some confidence and realize that you really can do a better job of this yourself. So, don't be intimidated.

So now you control this vital part of the sales process. You know which papers serve your area and are the most effective for marketing real estate; and now you know that most of these newspapers also have very cost effective online advertising.

In addition to online newspaper advertising, you need to make sure your property is listed for free on many of the real estate specific Internet sites. These include; www.FreeRealEstateOffice.com

www.FreeRealEstateOffice.com
www.aolrealestate.com
www.backpage.com
www.beatyouthere.com
www.canadahomeguide.ca
www.citycribs.com
www.clickablecitydirectory.com
www.clrsearch.com
www.condo.com
www.craigslist.com (can only be run for 30 days. Consider re-listing weekly)
www.cyberhomes.com
www.dothomes.com
www.ebay.com (advertising section separate from auction section)
www.facebook.com
www.flatfeeorders.com to find agents to list in MLS for A FEE
www.flatfeemlsdirect.com List in MLS for a fee
www.FreeRealEstateOffice.com
www.frontdoor.com
www.FSBO.com does flat fee MLS
www.googlebase.com spotlight ads are extra
www.homes.com
www.homescape.com
www.hotpads.com
www.house.com
www.inea.co.uk MLS like startup in UK
www.kijiji.com
www.lakehomesusa.com
www.landwatch.com
www.livedeal.com
www.local.com
www.military.com
www.myrealty.com
www.Nytimes.com
www.oodle.com

www.openhouse.com
www.owners.com also does flat fee MLS listing
www.PCSrealty.net Military
www.postlets.com
www.propbot.com
www.propertpreviews.com
www.realtor.com
www.secondspace.com
www.thehousingpages.com
www.trulia.com
www.uniqueglobalhomes.com
www.vast.com
www.videohomes.com
www.vivareal.us bilingual
www.walmart.com
www.WorldWide-RealEstate-ForSale.com international
www.wsj.com wall St. Journal online
www.yahoo.com
www.Youtube.com
www.zillow.com

At first this list may seem overwhelming but many of these Internet sites feed to one another. So once you place it in one it is then sent to others and it all starts to multiply.

One of the best places to start is with the flat fee services that get your property listed on the Multiple Listing Service. The cost for six months ranges from $275 to $600. These sites are only listing your property on MLS. There is no further commitment to pay them a commission but there is a commitment to cooperate and pay a buyers agent should they bring a buyer that completes a transfer of the property. The amount of commission paid is left totally up to the seller and at the time of the paperwork the seller must decide what percentage to offer to the buyer's agent. This amount should be ½ (one half) of what is normally paid for commissions in your area. Remember if a buyer comes direct, without an agent, then zero commission will be paid. So for a few hundred dollars you are saving at least one half of the commission.

The good part about this is that not only do you get all the MLS exposure it also gives you an MLS number for your property so that you can then get on almost any of the other sites. Each of these flat fee MLS listing sites will give you a list of all the other sites they feed to. After a few days check up on them and make sure the information is accurate. Then start after the other sites that your property is not on. Fill out the information sheets on these other sites and your listing will start to snowball because the new sites that you have used will also have feeds to other sites and your Internet coverage becomes viral. So by placing your property on 6 to 8 sites you will end up being included in almost all of them.

Another great way to advertise online is to check out using Google Adwords.

With the creation of a Google ADWORDS account, Google is letting you accomplish two things. The first is the placement of a very small four-line advertisement that they will paste up in several related categories and the other is the creation of a free web page.

Keep your information on the ad itself to the point. The first line is only 25 spaces long and should start out with city/town, state and price. The second and third lines are limited to 35 spaces each and again use abbreviations whenever possible and stick to the pertinent facts. Save the flowery descriptions for your new web page that has much more room for verbiage. The forth and last line in the ad automatically links or send anyone that clicks on your ad to the web page that can include a picture and or a map of the area.

What is critical to remember is that Google will only charge you when someone actually clicks on your ad to get more information about your property. Think of this as Google providing you with pre-screened leads of interested buyers.

The trick here is to be specific in both the first line of the ad and the keywords they shall ask you to pick out. Think of the keywords as a sort of directional finder that you want to keep as targeted as possible. Imagine that you are launching a missile and want to hit your property. You don't want to aim it at the key word "REAL ESTATE" because the category is so very broad that it may never hit your property. What you need to do is include your town/city and state in a combination or the keywords so that buyers interested in your area and product will have their sights narrowed down to that area. Avoid the individual use of the keyword "for sale." Instead use a combination of your city, state and the keyword to create a better target such as "Azusa, CA for sale". Avoid the keyword "real estate" but use "Azusa, Ca real estate," "Azusa, Ca property", "Azusa, Ca homes." These clear target keyword descriptions will save you from wasting money.

There are two different types of accounts Google will let you create. The standard and simplest account will ask you what you want to spend for a months worth of clicks. Try the minimum of $50 dollars and see what results you get.

A couple of reminders:

Whenever you list with any of these sites, it is critically important to go back online and review the information that they put up. Pay particular attention to sites like Zillow and others that publish an estimate of value. You need to make sure that their range of best guess value is not way off the mark, because they usually are and it can be detrimental to your sales efforts.

Remember to include the following phrase in all your advertising, "brokers protected" or "brokers welcome." This phrase will let all the real estate agents know that you are willing to work with them and their buyers and that you are willing pay them a commission.

You now realize that online advertising is inexpensive and often free. Hopefully, we have made it easy for you to use. So get out there and get your property online for the world to see.

Budget for Online and Open House Print Ads

The average price to advertise a property online in four of the major cities, every day for six months in two of the large regional newspapers, is approximately $22 per week. This is the average cost to be online in one of the largest regional newspapers and at the same time advertise online in a second large to medium newspaper. This survey included the cities of Los Angeles, Chicago, Boston and Miami. Chicago was the high at $30 a week and Los Angeles was the low.

It can be more expensive, but cost effective, if the placement is kept to Fridays or open house indexes is the placement of small print ads in these same large regional papers announcing an upcoming open house. The average price to run these ads in the same newspapers for nine weekends or every third weekend is approximately $36 per week.

That's a total budget of **$58 dollars a week** to advertise a property online every day and to also advertise open houses every third weekend in two major newspapers such as:

<u>Los Angeles</u>

- Los Angeles Times

- Los Angles Daily News

Chicago

- The Chicago Tribune

- The Chicago Sun Times

Boston

- The Boston Globe

- The Metro West Daily News

Miami

- Miami Herald

- Sun Sentinel

I recommend that when it comes to placing the open house or a small classified print ad for an open house, that you always call the newspaper. Newspapers are not very good at showing anything out side of multi-day packages over their Internet sites but they are usually available if you ask. Commonly they will have an open house section or index, but it is not mentioned online so you must call to be included in this section. Keep open house ads short and use abbreviations where possible.

An example open house ad will be similar to the following:

Open house
Sun 1-4, 15 Main St
Address
4Bd, 2 baths
$300,000
Brokers welcome

It is usually best to run the ad a day of two before the open house. For example, Friday for a Saturday open house and Friday and or Saturday for a Sunday open house. Keep away from the Sunday papers because they far more expensive and a serious buyer will be lining up their open house touring plans a day or two in advance and not likely the morning of.

If you spend some time online studying your market area newspapers, you will most probably find that many small to medium size publications will include tours of property online for free, but you need to make the call. How great an opportunity is this?

Remember to always include "brokers protected" or "brokers welcome" in your ads so that the buyer's brokers will know that you will pay them a commission for their efforts.

An additional $19 per week in the budget should be allowed for other incidental advertising such as enhanced Google ads, repositioning on Craig's list or other local online or print advertising.

This brings the **total advertising budget to $77 a week**. Compare this to a 5% or 6% commission and I think you will question why you would need to involve a listing realtor.

This stuff is simply not that hard or expensive to do on your own!

10. Showings are Easy

When it comes to showings, please relax!

In fact, showings are so easy to perform that most showings are led by complete strangers. Many Realtors showing a property through the Multiple Listing Service are entering that property for the very first time. They are not familiar with the property owner or a single thing about the property itself. Can you see the advantage that you, as the owner, already possess for the ability to show the property properly?

To demonstrate my point, think of the tried and true lock box system.

A lock box is used so that it is not necessary for a listing realtor to come to a property every time it needs to be shown and personally open up the doors for other realtors. Lock boxes are a devise that usually attach to the door handle and contain the key to that door. Any realtor who has the code to the lockbox can access the key and therefore access the property.

So with lockbox access, complete strangers enter the property with out any guidance whatsoever. And they make out perfectly fine.

During most showings, listing agents usually make themselves scarce and let the buyers and their agents feel their way around. It is usually better that way. They can and will talk freely amongst themselves about the property if the seller and seller's agents are not nearby within earshot.

The big national home developers have set up a maze system for showing their properties. Buyers are greeted by a salesperson when they first enter the model homes and then they are left alone to wonder and explore and most importantly discuss what works for them or what they would perhaps change. Then towards the end of a buyer's tour, they are led back into the waiting area containing friendly salespeople to take things to the next level.

So why be worried to hold a showing as the owner? The real fact is that showings are not showings at all. They are a group of strangers finding and discovering their way around an unfamiliar place.

The other important fact about showings that I must impress upon you is that the single most difficult part of showing a home is keeping it clean and presentable. With or without a listing realtor, the seller already does all of this behind the scenes heavy lifting and of cleaning the property. I do not know of any realtors out there who will clean and tidy up a home before they show it. The Seller performs this tough job. Always has and always will.

Another issue that is important to discuss is the need for sellers to relax about the condition of their property in order to show it. A seller will need to be concerned about of the possibility that a buyer will be coming in for a necessary look at any time. I realize that it is a difficult position to live in, and at the same time, keep your home in perfect condition at all times. But, life goes on and so do the everyday messes of a family. So try to relax by remembering that the buyers are coming to look at the structure and not how you keep house.

Think of showings this way. You, the owner/seller have always done the hard work of keeping the property presentable. It is now just a matter of changing who is opening the door to let buyers enter.

This is what you need to do

1. Keep the property as presentable as you can but remember that life goes on and no one lives in or expects perfection. Relax; the buyers have probably just left a home full of kids that I'll just bet is not as clean as the one you are trying to sell.

2. Print the property information sheets off of the website and leave then in a visible spot for potential buyers to take. Include plot plans and copies of photos for the buyers to take with them to show others.

3. Turn on every light you can find.

4. Unlock every door and lock

5. Get out of the way and stay out of the way! Don't hover around. Pick one or two station areas for yourself and hang out in that spot. If you are needed, I assure you that buyers will find you.

6. Remember, anything you say can and will be used against you. Stick to the facts about your property. Be honest, cordial and cheerful but limit the small talk too just small talk. No personal stories or information. Simple.

7. If you have aggressive pets, make arraignments for them. Perhaps you can keep them in the car for little while. Everyone thinks that their barking and or growling dog is fine because he or she has never ever hurt anyone, but you just might have let your animal chase away the best buyer that you were going to get. Don't risk it. Not everyone likes animals. Put away the dogs!

8. Any effort toward ambience is always helpful.

If you should desire one, the www.FreeRealEstateOffice.com allows for the use several types of lock box systems. It is a good way to go if you do not have any sensitive security issues and a no brainier if the property is empty.

Much has been said and written about staging your home for showings. If money is not an issue, then it is a fine way to help sell your property but generally I don't subscribe to this. Different people have different abilities, tastes and decor. Just do the best you can do to make it presentable. For some people, because of health issues or time constraints, even cleaning is impossible for them. Don't worry about it. As I started off this section telling you – houses show themselves and you never know what the buyer's vision is for the future of the property.

They will most probably alter, modernize, and change the property to fit their lifestyle and tastes.

The property is what it is and will sell for what it is, if priced properly and exposed fully to the market.

Think of showings this way, it is so that easy that complete strangers can show property (and they usually are.) There is absolutely no reason for you to get all geared up about showings either.

So you see, it's simple! Sellers have always done the heavy lifting in the showing process and they still do by keeping the property presentable.

11. Be Effective and Follow Up

The majority of prospective real estate buyers are searching the Internet for property. More than 80% of buyers use the Internet as a real estate shopping resource. That's an incredible number of buyers.

One of the best-kept secrets in today's real estate is that online newspaper advertising is extremely inexpensive and incredibly effective. You can place your house online, pictures and all, with major newspapers for about a buck a day. To go online in The Los Angeles Times costs $99.00 for 90 days. The Boston Globe has a special of $199.00 until the property sells. You just cannot afford to ignore these rates.

So, most buyers are looking online and to get online in front of them is cheap but the one thing that you need to know and respect is that online buyers for any product or service expect quick responses to information requests.

If you go online with your product (property) you need to respond to people right away. I am not saying you need to constantly baby-sit the phone and drop everything at a moments notice. You just need to respond in a reasonable amount of time. However, I must caution you that if there is something in your life that would preclude you from this critical step than you should refrain from going online to sell. If you don't follow up effectively, someone else will.

So many real estate agents are guilty of this crime. Don't make this same mistake.

The last statistic that I saw concerning the average response time that it takes for an agent to respond to a buyer's inquiry for information was 72 hours! From my experience, that's if I receive a response from a broker at all. That's three full days! And this is just the average. Half of the responses take even longer than three days. A lot can change in three days. A buyer might see other properties for an entire weekend and purchase something else, when in fact they might have preferred your property if they had only received the requested information in a timely manner from the listing agent. Do you have any idea how many other properties a buyer may have seen from other more efficient responses?

With the right tools at hand, sellers can and will do a better job than the majority of realtors. How hard is it to respond to someone that wants to buy your property, when after all, you want to sell and they want to buy?

In this "do it now" society what information do we wait three days for? Maybe for medical results but as a society we don't wait long for information and why should we, when the Internet and computers put so much at our fingertips we want and expect more.

I recently attempted to help some friends of mine with a piece of land they own in Savannah, Georgia. My friends are from out of state and this land is a problem in their lives. So I offered to help and find an effective Savannah broker to sell the property. I created a test in which I was a buyer seeking just the same type of commercial land that my friends want to sell. I spoke by phone live with seven different commercial agents from seven different companies and I left a message for the eighth. Each and every one of these commercial, professional agents promised to get back to me with the target properties that I specified. I made my needs and requests simple to fill. Weeks later, one agent got back to me with information. One out of eight! Are they that busy in Savannah? Somehow I do not think so! Brokers and agents manage, or shall I say mismanage, trillions of dollars of real property assets and this is a prime example of this mismanagement.

One of the largest real estate companies in the American market has a computer system that they have developed to keep their agents efficient at following up on buyer's requests for information. If an agent does not take the call they immediately, he or she loses this potential customer. Then, within eight hours the agent needs to respond to this computer watchdog about their actions performed or they are removed from the system. Now, this company will brag and show a potential seller how fast their agents respond to an inquiry about your property. But the real truth is that they created this system to weed out their poorly responding agents. They don't want to get rid of these unresponsive agents altogether; they just merely want to remove them from high priority situations. This company has a watchdog system to keep their agents feet to the fire and respond as society expects. Trillions of dollars worth of real property is in these people's hands and without a watchdog the response is dismal.

I can't tell you the number of times that I have responded to a newspaper advertisement or called a phone number pasted on a sign only to have my contact left unanswered.

It just amazes me. Do you know of another type product or industry where the buyer's response, generated by costly advertising, remains completely ignored? Corporations and businesses of all sizes and descriptions spend money on advertising to generate interest in their product. Then they effectively respond to that interest and try to sell the product that was advertised. Any type of product follows this chain reaction from cars, makeup, pharmaceuticals, and appliances to computers, with the single exception real estate. Real estate companies of all sizes spend huge money on advertising to create interest. Then, maybe just maybe, someone responds to the buyer's interest! Can you think of any product that is mismanaged like real estate? And the sad part about the whole thing is that out of all the products out there, this product just so happens to be most people's single largest asset. If this were another type of product, heads would roll in corporate America for behavior even remotely similar to what takes place in the real estate industry.

I recently responded and left a message regarding a property advertised in a large professional real estate paper. It was a sizable advertisement in an industry specific professional newspaper for several hundred acres of land abutting a large interstate highway. I never heard back from any agent at this firm.

This advertisement had to cost someone quite a bit of money. If the land had been placed on deposit, the agent is crazy not to want to identify me as someone looking for large land parcels, to see if I might have interest as a potential back-up buyer or perhaps to look at some other land parcels. If you had happened to be the owner of this land, now that you are aware that calls about your land remain unanswered, would you still employ this agent or this company to handle the disposition of your major asset?

This was not a unique situation. This happens all the time. Is it happening to your real estate? How do you know?

If you become the one responsible for responding to the advertising that you have spent money on, then I guarantee that you would surely know if inquires are being efficiently returned.

This is an advanced system for your benefit. It will help you to sell faster and better, but you need to pick up the phone or email back to people. Don't by shy. Don't worry about if it's too late at night. Your primary job is to respond.

You have spent energy and money placing on-line ads. Review your hits, return your emails and schedule your appointments. It costs you money to generate interest in your property, so be effective and efficient. This system is designed to make it easy for you.

I implore you to be efficient and respond! It's just not that hard or time consuming!

12. All Information Concerning the Property Becomes the Property of the Property.

This system includes releases and requires every professional and company involved in the transaction to cooperate and send any and all information and documents pertaining to the property and transaction to the property filing cabinet. Regardless of who has purchased or generated this information, it needs to be sent and filed in the property filing cabinet that is accessible to the seller.

This is a standard blanket type of agreement that applies to every property for sale on the system. This agreement is to be executed by a potential buyer before they can submit an offer to purchase. This way there is no confusion. It applies to every property and needs to be executed before hand.

The reasoning behind this is that until you actually transfer the title to your property, until the property is actually owned by another, you do not know what usefulness or value any of these documents may have for you. This is especially true for the next transaction if this transaction should fall through. And any and all of this information is entirely unique to your certain real estate and no other. There is no other value for these documents, they do not concern any other real estate in the universe expect yours and the information should run with the property.

If you have performed all the inspections that the buyer should request that you perform, but and at the buyer's expense, additional inspections or testing is requested, do not be alarmed. Go ahead and let the buyers proceed. The buyers need to satisfy themselves as to the exact nature of what they are purchasing and it is a reasonable request. But now, because of this information sharing agreement, the entire report must be electronically sent through the website to the property information filing cabinet before it can be discussed. The agreement also states that should the buyer not perform and complete the transaction, for any reason, this information becomes the property of the seller and can be used by the seller and at the seller's sole discretion.

Why is this necessary? Suppose this inspection shows something critical that your inspection did not. You will need this document to file a claim against your inspector. Or worse you lose the sale because of this new information. You now have a more exact picture about the true nature of your property based on both inspections and can therefore make new decisions based upon these combined set of facts.

Let's look at another example.

The buyer's application process for financing will always involve the performance of an appraisal. If for some reason your sale should fall through, you now have a professional's opinion of value for your review or for you to use as basis for your price that can be shared with any subsequent buyer.

This can hold true with all sorts of other types of plans or documents that all pertain uniquely to your property. Perhaps your sale includes the subdivision of land. There will be numerous reports, applications, plans and engineering generated about your property. As the seller, you need to be copied on these as they are assembled. This will avoid any issues with tiring to obtain them at a later date if there should be any problems.

Expect and attempt to avoid the unexpected.

EXAMPLE ONLY

Not to be used as a legal document

OFFER TO PURCHASE REAL ESTATE

Date: _____

To: _____

    (Seller)

_____

_____

Real Property known and numbered as:

_____

_____

_____

Land consisting of _____ acres more or less.

More particularly described in a deed(s) dated_____,
_____ in the Municipal, County or State records in Deed book
number_____, Page number_____.

I will pay $_____, for above described real
property. Of which

       $ _____ is paid herewith as a deposit
to bind this offer

$ _____ is to be paid as an additional deposit upon the execution of the Purchase and Sale Agreement.

$ _____ is to be paid at the delivery of the Deed.

$ _____

====================

Total Purchase Price $ _____

This offer is good until _____ A.M. / P.M. on _____, 20___. On or before this time a copy of this offer needs to signed by the Seller if accepted, if not accepted by such time this offer is deemed null and void and all deposit monies will be returned to the Buyer.

The parties hereto shall execute a Purchase and Sale Agreement on or before _____, 20___. Upon execution this agreement will encompass the entire agreement between the parties hereto.

A good and sufficient Deed, conveying clear and marketable title shall be delivered on _____,20___ at a mutually agreed upon location.

If the Buyer(s) does not fulfill their obligations under this offer, the deposit shall become the Seller(s) property without recourse. Said deposit shall be held by (circle one and cross off others) Seller, Seller's Attorney, SafeFunds or Escrow. Subject to the terms contained herein.

Additional Provisions: (if none state NONE) _____

_____

_____

_____

_____

_____

_____

_____

Disclosures: Buyer acknowledges receipt of inspection(s) performed by others for the Seller. Subject to any additional provisions and/or any inspection/tests that will be performed at the Buyers expense with copies of results given to the Seller and made a part of this agreement.

Mortgage Contingency: This agreement is contingent upon the Buyer obtaining a mortgage commitment without conditions in the amount of $_____, amortized for a term of _____years at prevailing interest rates. Buyer agrees to apply for a mortgage within ___ days of seller's acceptance. If Buyer fails to make formal application by said date, Buyer shall be in default of this agreement and shall forfeit all deposit monies. Mortgage Commitment shall be obtained on or before _____, 20___. It is further agreed that if, after diligent effort, the Buyer is unable to obtain the mortgage by said commitment date, then all deposits shall be returned to the Buyer, provided the Seller has received written notice from Buyer with proof of said inability within five (5) business days after said commitment date, and this agreement will become null and void.

Commission: The Real Estate Broker involved in this transaction is (if none state NONE) _____
_____. Seller agrees to pay a real estate commission of ___% to this and only this Broker if, as and when the transfer of deed is fully completed and all monies to the seller have been paid.

Electronic Record: The Parties Agree that they shall make use an electronic record, including facsimile or e-mail, to make, bind and keep this agreement. Either party has a right to withdraw consent to the use of electronic record provided they state so before the execution of this agreement. Neither party has the right to withdraw consent to this agreement made by electronic record once it has been signed.

The Seller's electronic address is:

( ) E-mail address _____
     or
( ) Facsimile number _____

The Buyer's or Buyer's agents electronic address is:

( ) E-mail address _____
     or
( ) Facsimile number _____

Time is of the essence.

NOTICE: This is intended to be a legal document that creates binding obligations. If it is not completely understood, consult an Attorney.

_____   _____
Buyer   Buyer

_____
Address

_____

_____
Phone Number

This offer is hereby accepted upon the foregoing terms and condition at _____A.M./P.M. on _____, 20___.

_____   _____
Seller   Seller

EXAMPLE ONLY

Not to be used as a legal document

PURCHASE AND SALE AGREEMENT

Seller(s) _____

Address _____

Buyer(s) _____

Address _____

Seller agrees to sell and Buyer agrees to purchase certain real property
known and numbered as _____

_____, _____, _____.

More particularly described in a deed(s) dated_____,

_____ in the Municipal, County or State records in Deed book

number_____, Page number_____.

The Land consisting of _____ acres more or less.

1. PURCHASE PRICE

The agreed purchase price of the premises is

The Sum of _____DOLLARS$_____

Payable as follows:

By deposit, subject to collection----------------------$_____

Additional deposit due by _____, 20___. (if none state
NONE)If not received by seller on or before said date buyer shall be
in default.--$_____

Proceeds from institutional financing
(if none state NONE)---------------------------------$_____

Balance by cash, bank check or trustee check
at transfer of deed----------------------------------$_____

2. MORTGAGE CONTINGENCIES:

This agreement is contingent upon the Buyer obtaining a mortgage commitment without conditions in the amount of (if a cash sale state NONE) $_____, amortized for a term of ____years at prevailing interest rates. Buyer agrees to apply for a conventional bank or other institutional mortgage loan within ___ days of seller's acceptance. If Buyer fails to make formal application by said date, Buyer shall be in default of this agreement and shall forfeit all deposit monies. Time is of the essence. The Mortgage Commitment shall be obtained on or before _____, _____. It is further agreed that if, after diligent effort, the Buyer is unable to obtain the mortgage by said commitment date, then all deposits shall be returned to the Buyer, provided the Seller has received written notice from Buyer with proof of said inability within five (5) business days after said commitment date, and this agreement will become null and void. In the event Seller has not received said notice then this mortgage contingency shall be deemed satisfied. *Buyer grants permission to their lending institution to provide complete loan status information to the Seller upon the Sellers request.*

3. ESCROW DEPOSIT:

All deposits shall be payable to Seller (or Seller's attorney, Safefunds or escrow agent) _____ as here agreed to between the parties. At the time of the transfer of the deed said holder of deposit monies shall pay the deposit funds to the Seller. If the Buyer shall fail to make any deposit funds payable pursuant to this agreement, Seller may declare the Buyer in default and terminate this agreement and Seller shall be relieved of all obligations contained in this agreement. Seller may give written notice to Buyer by certified mail to this effect after such default.

4. CLOSING: (TRANSFER OF DEED)

The Seller shall deliver to the Buyer a good, sufficient deed (Warranty or Quitclaim), conveying a good clear marketable title, on or before the _____ day of _____, 20___.

5. INSPECTION OF PREMISES and CONDITION:

The property and improvements are to be conveyed in their present condition, free from all tenants, subject to reasonable wear and use, as they are on the date of this agreement. The Buyer represents that the Buyer has examined said property and is satisfied with the condition thereof, subject to additional inspections and tests that are made a part of this Agreement. Buyer further agrees that Seller has not made any representations or promises other than those expressly stated herein. The Seller does not warrant and is not required to repair cosmetic conditions. The Buyer has the right to make a final inspection of the property prior to the transfer of the deed to verify that the Seller has made any agreed upon repairs and that the property is in the same condition as it was at the signing of this agreement. If the Buyer fails to perform this inspection, Seller's obligations shall be deemed to have been satisfied. Seller will cooperate fully and give Buyers inspectors and experts full access to the property for said inspections.

6. FIXTURES AND PERSONAL PROPERTY:

Unless otherwise agreed to in writing hereto the premises to be conveyed shall include built-ins such as but not limited to dishwasher, oven/range/stove, microwave, etc; garage door opener(s) and remote control(s); plumbing, lighting, heating fixtures; screens, storm doors, storm windows; TV/cable antennas; wall to wall carpeting; awnings; plants and shrubbery.

And the following described personal property: _____

_____

_____

_____

_____

7. ENCUMBRANCES:

Unless otherwise noted the property will be conveyed free and clear of liens and encumbrances, except: Provisions of any local zoning laws, if any; ordinance, municipal regulation, public or private law agreements, restrictions and easements of record, and facts disclosed by inspection of the property, provided they do not affect marketability and do not unreasonably interfere with Buyer's use of said premises.

8. ADJUSTMENTS:

Unless otherwise agreed to in this agreement, all adjustments of taxes for the then current fiscal year, water, sewer, fuel oil, interest, condominium fees, rents, etc., Shall be apportioned as of the date of transfer of the deed and the net amount thereof shall be added to or deducted from, as the case may be, the purchase price payable by the Buyer at the time of said transfer of the deed.

9. OCCUPANCY:

On the date and time of the property transfer, The Seller shall deliver full possession and occupancy of said property to the Buyer. The premises shall be free from all occupants, possessions, personal property and in a broom clean condition.

10. DEFAULT:

If Legal action is brought to enforce any provisions of this agreement, the prevailing party shall be entitled to court costs and reasonable attorney's fees.

If the Buyer should default on this agreement the Seller shall retain the deposit money as liquidated damages.

If the Seller should default on this agreement the Buyer shall reclaim the deposit money as liquidated damages and this shall be the Buyers sole remedy at law or in equity.

11. RISK OF LOSS:

The risk of loss to the property by fire, theft, acts of god or other casualty until the delivery of the deed shall be upon the seller. In the event of loss or damage that cannot be repaired before the delivery of the deed then the Buyer shall have the choice of either receiving the benefit and insurance proceeds from the Seller's insurance company and taking title, or reclaiming the deposit monies and voiding this agreement and all parties shall be relieved of further liability.

12. ADDITIONAL PROVISIONS:

_____

_____

_____

_____

_____

_____

_____

_____

_____

_____

_____

_____

_____

13. **COMMISSION:**

The Real Estate Broker involved in this transaction is (if none state NONE) _____ .

Seller agrees to pay a real estate commission of ___% to this and only this Broker if, as and when the transfer of deed is fully completed and all monies to the seller have been paid. Buyer and Seller mutually warrant and represent that neither has dealt with a real estate broker or salesperson in connection with this transaction, other than referenced above, and that neither was directed to the other by any other agent or broker, and each agrees to indemnify and hold harmless against all costs, damages, expense or liability, including attorneys fees, incurred by the other arising out of or resulting from breach of this warranty or failure of this representation. The Provision of this paragraph shall survive delivery of the deed.

14. **ASSIGNMENT and SURVIVORSHIP:**

This agreement shall be binding upon the heirs, executors, administrators, successors and assigns of the parties hereto. This agreement may be assigned by either party without the written consent of the other but may not be assigned without the express consent of the Seller, if it contains a provision for Seller financing.

15. CONSTRUCTION OF AGREEMENT:

This agreement is executed electronically or in multiple counterparts, is to be construed as a (name of particular State) _____ contract, is to take effect as a sealed instrument, sets forth the entire contract between the parties, is binding upon the enures to the parties hereto and their respective heirs, devises, executors, administrators, successors and assigns, and may be cancelled, modified or amended only by a written instrument executed by both the Seller and the Buyer. If two or more persons are named herein as the Buyer their obligations hereunder shall be joint and several. The captions and marginal notes are used only as a matter of convenience and are not to be considered a part of this agreement or to be used in determining the intent of the parties to it.

16. EXTENTION TO PERFECT TITLE OR MAKE PREMOSES CONFORM:

If the Seller is unable to give clear title or to make the conveyance, or to deliver possession of the premises, all as herein stipulated, or if at the time of transfer of the deed the premises do not conform with the provisions hereof, then the Seller shall use reasonable efforts to remove any defects in title or deliver possession as provided herein, or to make the premises conform to the provisions hereof, and thereupon the tire for transfer shall be extended for a period of thirty (30) days. If at the end of the thirty days the Seller cannot make the premises conform, then the deposit made under this agreement shall be forthwith refunded and all obligations of the parties hereto shall cease and this agreement shall be null and void without recourse to the parties hereto.

17. BUYER'S ELECTION TO ACCEPT TITLE:

The Buyer shall have the election, at either the original or any extended transfer to accept such title as the Seller can deliver to the said premises in their then condition and to pay therefore the purchase price without deduction, in which case the Seller shall convey such title.

18. **USE OF MONEY TO CLEAR TITLE:**

The Seller may, at the transfer of title, use the purchase money or any portion thereof to clear the title of any or all encumbrances, provided that all instruments releasing such encumbrances are recorded simultaneously with the transfer of the deed or arrangements satisfactory to the Buyer and Buyer's mortgagee are made for the recording of such instruments within a reasonable period after the transfer.

19. **USE of ELECTRONIC RECORD:**

The Parties Agree that they shall make use an electronic record, including facsimile or e-mail, to make, bind and keep this agreement. Either party has a right to withdraw consent to the use of electronic record provided they state so before the execution of this agreement. Neither party has the right to withdraw consent to this agreement made by electronic record once it has been signed.

The Seller's electronic address is:

( ) E-mail address _____
     or
( ) Facsimile number _____

The Buyer's or Buyer's agents electronic address is:

( ) E-mail address _____
     or
( ) Facsimile number _____

20. ENTIRE AGREEMENT:

This agreement and attached addenda (if any), represents the entire agreement between the parties. It shall not be changed orally but only by a written instrument, which is signed by all parties hereto and supercedes all prior negotiations, representations or agreements either written or oral. The effective date of this Agreement shall be the date on which all signatures, and initials (if any), have been affixed hereto.

Time is of the essence.

NOTICE: This is intended to be a legal document that creates binding obligations. If it is not completely understood, consult an attorney prior to signing.

_____   _____
Buyer   Buyer

_____
Address

_____

_____
Phone Number

This offer is hereby accepted upon the foregoing terms and condition at ____A.M./P.M. on _____, 20____.

_____   _____
Seller   Seller

PART III

Other Advice

The End of the Information Dinosaur

Through the use of the property filing cabinet on <u>www.</u> <u>FreeRealEstateOffice.com</u>, sellers are able to get status updates on the buyer's mortgage efforts simply and easily without the annoying need to place phone calls and wait for overdue answers.

In order for buyers to submit an offer on any property they must agree and commit to instruct their lending institution to update the property specific filing cabinet on a daily basis of any all changes and milestones in the loan process.

The first information posted by the lender will need to take place within the first 3-5 days subsequent to the acceptance of the offer.

This information will state pertinent information such as:

- Name and address of lender
- Name and contact information of loan officer
- Actual date of application was submitted
- Agreement all information of loan will be submitted to the property filing cabinet and if agreement is breached it creates cause that can nullify sales agreement.
- Provide list of action items necessary by buyer
- Provide list of expected milestone dates

- Expected commitment date
- Approval or denial
- Approval with conditions
- Commitment expiration date
- Closing date

Remember, it is very important that you, as the seller, know exactly how your potential sale stands. The potential borrower's financial condition and speed of application and the status of the application process are the first tangible results that you will have to judge whether you are on the right track with a particular buyer. You don't want to have your property off the market for a shaky or dead deal any longer than humanly possible. Time costs you money and wasting precious time by taking your real estate off the market for buyers who cannot get financing should be avoided.

The communication ability that is offered on www.FreeRealEstateOffice.com frees the seller from the abyss of the information black hole and allows the seller to enter the twenty-first century.

THE BLACK HOLE

The "current conflict system" places the seller in a situation in which the issue of financing disappears into a black hole and the seller waits, wonders and worries what is taking place with the buyer's loan and how is it progressing.

This is the single largest and most time consuming hurdle most transactions need to cross and for most sellers it becomes a black hole where little or any actual information has been made available to them.

Let's look at the current dinosaur communications that take place when a seller wants an update on the buyer's mortgage status with the "current conflict system."

1. The seller needs to call the seller's listing agent and ask a concerned question such as; it's been 3 weeks have the buyers received the mortgage commitment yet?

2. Listing agent calls buyer's agent

3. Buyer's agent calls buyer

4. Buyer calls bank and leaves message

5. Loan officer calls buyer back

6. Buyer calls buyer's agent back
7. Buyer's agent calls seller's listing agent back
8. Listing agent informs seller of status

Eight phone calls were necessary for the seller to receive this vital answer. How many days can and do transpire for this chain reaction of calls to return the requested information? If all five of these separate entities efficiently perform their jobs and returned the proper calls in a timely manner, this dinosaur communication process can take several days. If there is only one bad link in this chain then the true answer may never be obtained.

Today kids' cell phones can update them about what their entire chain of friends are discussing in an instant, but the seller of several hundreds of thousands of dollars in real estate is kept in the dark like Mayberry RFD because the National Association of Realtors is frightened that sellers will gain too much control if they modernize the sales process and are allowed to utilize technology.

FINANCING

Most Real Estate purchases involve the need for financing. Usually the transaction is contingent upon the buyer being able to obtain a certain percentage of financing at prevailing interest rates and terms by a date certain, usually within 30 days.

Not only this, but there should also be an additional clause which gives the buyer a very short amount of time to apply for the loan, usually only 3 to 5 business days from the acceptance of the offer. This is all the time a serious buyer will need in order to get to a lender and start the lengthy paperwork process needed to obtain a mortgage. This is an extremely good practice and not all real estate agents demand it, but it must be done because it almost instantly separates out buyers that are completely serious about the purchase and prevents the others from unnecessarily removing the property from the market for any damaging length of time.

So in effect, the property is off the market for a quick 3-5 days and then if the buyer has proven that they are serious they get an additional 25 days for the lender to complete the loan process. The property should, at the longest point, only be off the market for one month while all of the contingencies are being satisfied. After the one-month period for financing, the transaction should now be in a waiting pattern with no outstanding obstacles to overcome until the closing takes place.

PRE-QUALIFICATION LETTERS

I do not know if it was the real estate sales community or the lending industry that was responsible for inventing the usage of pre-qualification letters, but whoever it was should be shot. The use of these is perhaps one of the single biggest disservices to ever happen to the real estate seller.

Pre-qualification letters are a worthless statement that can be provided by almost anyone and can and do deceive sellers into believing that the buyer presenting them has a great chance to obtain a mortgage. Nothing more, they can be prepared by anyone and they do not contain any substance. Information provided by the buyer is not substantiated in any shape or form. The buyer can claim or even believe that they are credit worthy when in fact they are not, or the buyer can state their income is high enough to pay back the mortgage when they cannot. Nothing the buyer claims is investigated or proven, it is simply taken at face value and used to spit out a "pre-qual" letter (as brokers refer to them as) that does not carry any weight. "Pre-qual" letters are completely worthless and a seller should not remove their property from the market under the false sense of security they create.

PRE-APPROVAL LETTERS

Pre-approval letters carry much more weight than the pre-qualification letters mentioned earlier.

A pre-approval letter has been provided to a buyer from a certain financial institution that is familiar with the buyer and either has knowledge of or has investigated the buyer's ability to secure the necessary financing.

The best type of pre-approval will have no conditions to be met other than the buyer's actual selection of a property in the price range that the bank has committed to.

Sellers still need to scrutinize these letters to make sure that they do not contain any strange stipulations or conditions. Some of these can be more like the worthless pre-qualification letters uses by some banks so be careful and read the fine print before you get excited that you have found a good buyer.

One other word of caution is to make certain that if you accept an offer from a buyer with a loan pre-approval letter, make sure that this buyer actually goes back to that same lending institution to complete the transaction. If they should switch to another lender than this pre-approval will become worthless because the buyers shall need to start at the beginning of the loan process.

A good pre-approval letter should also shorten the time a buyer needs on their financing contingency.

COMMITMENT LETTERS

Commitment letters are the complete opposite of a pre-qualification letter. Think of them more like a post qualification letter. Everything about the applicant's finances has been investigated and proven to conform to the lenders standards. The lender has actually committed to lend the funds necessary for the buyer to complete the transaction on a date certain.

When the seller gives the buyer 30 days to obtain financing, this is what the buyer should come back to the seller with as proof that they are good to go to complete the entire transaction.

Sellers need to scrutinize the actual commitment letter to make sure it does not contain conditions. If it does have conditions then it is not a firm commitment, it is a conditional commitment. Only a commitment letter without conditions is acceptable. A conditional commitment is considered unacceptable. At this point a seller will need to make one of several possible decisions:

- Give the buyer more time to satisfy the conditions

- Place the property back on the market with the understanding that if the buyer remedies the situation they are welcome to come back to the pervious deal

- Void the transaction and place the property back on the market.

Deposits

The way deposits are handled under the "Current Conflict System" is completely and utterly ridiculous. This current system is truly a dinosaur rattling about in the PayPal era.

What is now commonly done with deposits in co-brokered sales is that the buyer will write out a deposit check and then give it to their realtor along with a signed offer to purchase. The buyer's realtor will then fax or scan a copy of the check along with a copy of the offer to purchase to the seller's agent. The seller's agent will discuss the offer with the seller and then a counteroffer or several counteroffers may take place. While this is all happening, usually over several days, the check remains in the buyer's agent's folder or desk. The check is still only a piece of paper, a mere representation of what is supposed to be a good faith offer. It is not cash. It has not been cashed. It has no actual value and does not prove that the buyer even has the amount to cover the stated value. Once the offer has been accept this check will be turned over to someone on the Sellers side of the equation. It is not until this check actually clears the bank where it is now located (several days or weeks later) that it represents a real deposit. Until this happening the deposit has been show and tell. In all likelihood your property may be off the market this entire time of negotiations for a worthless, unsubstantiated piece of paper.

You cannot place a $100.00 deposit on a $2,000.00 car on Ebay without the deposit money being proven to actually exist and be authenticated as real money. Why then does the National Association of Realtors pretend that a deposit on a $200,000.00 property should be handled with any less force and effect than a $2,000.00 car on Ebay?

Depending upon which state your property is located in, once a basic understanding through the offer is reached between the parties, a longer more formal Purchase and Sale Agreement will be prepared, usually by the seller's attorney and at that time an additional deposit shall be due.

This deposit money will still be symbolic in nature because most transactions have some sort of contingencies, such as a need for financing, that are as yet unmet. But while the deposit is only symbolic, it should be verified from the very beginning that it does in fact represent that the buyer does indeed possess that amount of money and that the seller will someday be entitled to it when the contingencies are met

On www.FreeRealEstateOffice.com all offers are submitted online and at the sellers' discretion, deposits can be instantly verified and placed in a neutral escrow bank account to verify that the funds are good. These fund can be held until all contingencies are met or until the actual closing. Other options for the deposit monies that must be agreed upon in advance are the holding of the deposit money or option money directly by the seller, the seller's attorney, title company or an escrow company.

From the very onset of negotiations deposit money is now real and not just a piece of paper stuffed in a drawer.

Amount of Good Faith Deposit

What is the correct amount of a deposit?

Although it will actually be the bank or lender that has all their pertinent information about the buyer, and in the final analysis they make the decisions, on a preliminary basis you need to size up the buyer and his or her deposit or lack of deposit money will give you some insight. If the buyer is tight on funds do not become disillusioned. Tight on money is much different than no money. Don't throw the baby out with the bath water. Tight on money just means that you need to keep a shorter leash on your buyer by controlling the clock and giving them tight timelines to follow. This will monitor the buyers and give them less of a chance to waste your precious time and money.

What you are trying to accomplish with a deposit is two-fold.

1. Prove that you are not taking your property off the market unnecessarily.

2. Establish that the buyers have enough money to perform or consummate the transaction.

So how do you judge what is an adequate amount for a deposit?

One school of though is to set a figure that the average person would not easily walk away from if they should happen to change their minds and want to back out of the transaction at the last moment for no other valid reason.

Another is to request a percentage of the sale price. This amount is usually somewhere between 5 to 10% of the purchase price. On higher priced properties the terms can vary considerably. If you are the slightest bit concerned review **principal #4** and ask your lawyer.

Remember you are not selling a $5,000.00 used car. The deposit should reflect the size of the sale.

Signs

How many times have you seen a for sale sign leaning over, broken, faded and hard to read, dirty from age, the elements or even snowplows.

From the buyer's viewpoint, this sign is a first impression and you know what they say about first impressions. What is the message that this poor signage gives to a potential buyer and what does it tell the buyer about the seller or the property? Neglect that no one cares about the sign and perhaps no one cares about the property either. The property has been for sale so long that the sign looks old. Perhaps because the property has been for sale for so long, that the seller will be finally ready to take a low price. Or the seller is so incapable of maintaining the sign maybe they are incapable of maintaining the property as well.

There is no good conclusion that a buyer can have from bad signage.

Maybe the sign looks so bad and faded that the buyers completely dismiss the property as being no longer for sale and look at other more active properties. Perhaps they feel that if no one cares about the condition of the sign then maybe the same is true about the condition of the property.

From the seller's standpoint, a seller could ask and question the realtor's efforts. Either the agent has not been to the property in quite some time or perhaps he or she is too lazy to fix and replace the sign, or is it that he or she simply does not care. Either way the interpretation is not healthy.

Do not make this same mistake. Set the tone of your property sale right up front with your signage. If you self market, let the sign show prospective buyers and their agents that:

- You are confident, you have the ability to self market

- You are professional with a quality sign

- You are not cheap, you are capable

- You are serious

- You are on top of the process

- You care for the property

If your property is located where there are extreme elements or where the signage might be subjected to theft, it is always a good idea to keep a spare sign on hand so that the property is never without representation. I t is also wise to consider directional signs as well as open house signs and any include and aspects unique to the property such as waterfront or large acreage, etc.

Signage is available on the www.FreeRealEstateOffice.com located in the supply room. There are different types of signs to choose from and they are customizable to the seller's requirements. Besides size and shape, seller's can select how their contact information is to be shown.

HOLDING YOUR OWN OPEN HOUSE

Similar to having a showing, an open house is another one of the areas where the seller does most of the work anyway. The seller is the one who cleans the property so it is in its most presentable condition for strangers to enter.

So relax; it's easy! You already do all the heavy lifting whether an agent is involved or not!

A showing or an open house is mostly about making sure the property looks its best. Decide what dates you want to have the open house and, at least one week in advance, call your local newspaper or papers and run small print ads (keep it cost effective). The ad should include the address, price and a short description of the property. You can also modify your newspaper online advertising to include the open house as well. Then on the day of the open house, about one half hour before it is to start, place the open house signs at strategic locations to direct the traffic to your property. Remember to turn on every light that you can find and unlock all the doors. Print out the property fact sheets and a copy of the home inspection report and leave them in an obvious place; the kitchen countertop works well.

It is that simple. Open up the property to buyers and the buyer's agents and then make yourself scarce. Be present but locate yourself in an out of the way spot. Don't worry and hover about the buyers. If they should need you or have a question they will find you and ask.

Keep in mind principle # 6 that you want to be courteous and friendly but limit your conversation to small talk and property specific information. Your personal business can and will cost you money if it is shared too freely. You are selling because it is a good time in your life to sell. This reason or something like it is all you need to share. Please avoid using the worn out excuse "that you do not need to sell." Everyone and their brother uses this excuse and it does not sound credible.

One other note, please do not be discouraged if you do not get a lot of traffic through the property. Realtors state all the time that open houses are not worth it. Maybe that's good for them, but keep in mind that all it takes is one buyer and that's all you are looking for. Just one buyer and any open house is a success.

OLD PHOTOS

Have you ever looked thru MLS in the summertime and seen pictures of property for sale with the snow on the ground?

This mistake by realtors screams out loud and clear: "I've been for sale for a very long time." This can leads buyers to one of several conclusions and none of them are good.

Take full advantage of every photo opportunity for your property. If the particular Internet site allows for 25 photographs then put in 25 photographs. You say your property is small and you cannot find 25 things to take pictures of. Give the camera to someone else and they can take the pictures for you. If you can't find someone then get creative and take close-ups of details such as door trim, cabinetry, inside closets, inside showers, or widows. People go to the Internet sites to make it easy on themselves by seeing the property in advance. So show them what you have for sale. Pretend that your property is a politician and use every photo opportunity you can get.

If the pictures are on the outside keep your photos current with the seasons. You can even play up the seasons with certain festivities and customs.

Final Walk-Thru

After everything is complete and there are no outstanding contingencies that could alter the sales process, several days before the transfer of the deed is to take place, some buyers may want to have a final walk-thru of the property. This item should have been brought up when terms (P&S Agreement) were negotiated, but if it was not it is not uncommon for the seller to allow this. A walk-thru is a very reasonable request, but the scope of the review needs to be agreed upon beforehand so there are no surprises.

The reason a scope of the final walk-thru needs to be established is to make sure the walk thru does not become a nit-pick session. Perhaps you have agreed to fix certain defects or perform certain repairs that were highlighted in the home inspection. The property should be in substantially the same condition it was when the agreements to sell were executed. A two year old house is a fairly young house, but an 8 year old house with 8 year old paint that now that is now empty of the furniture and decorations will look very old and dated. The buyer has to expect some of this and you need not redo this type of wear and tear items unless you have previously agreed to perform this, in writing, as part of your agreements

If the condition has changed after the buyers saw the property and agreed to purchase the property, the seller needs to made good and return the property to the condition that existed at time of agreement. Perhaps, subsequent to the buyers last visit there was an accident and someone dented a garage door. The seller needs to repair or replace this door to the same or better condition that existed at the time of agreement or notify the buyer and the seller's attorney so an adjustment can be made at the closing. It's only fair.

If it is a re-sale house that you are transferring, it is only reasonable for the buyers to expect that the real estate is left free of all personal property, trash and belongings inside and out. There are few things on earth any more disgusting than someone else's personal waste or mess. The toilets, showers, refrigerator, and the like, need to be left clean for the next owners.

It is only common decency.

Do not assume the next owner wants anything but the empty real estate. If you are trying to be kind and leave something of value behind for the next owners always ask beforehand. Remember your stuff is nothing but junk to the next guy.

Also, try to perform the final walk-thru a couple of days in advance of the closing. This leaves time for any outstanding issues to be resolved.

PART IV

Real Estate 3.0

www.FreeRealEstateOffice.com

A completely new real estate sales system is now available on www. **FreeRealEstateOffice.com.** Real Estate 3.0 has been created to help sellers market their properties with more control, faster, better and for less money than ever before.

The Free Real Estate Office replaces the expense, conflict and problems of listing brokers by using new systems on the Internet. Information services and sales tools are online at your own property specific sales and information office. For the first time sellers have full access to an organized system that gives them complete control all the way through the entire sales process. Up to the minute answers and exact information are reported directly to you. Every entity, involved in your transaction will now report to you about the property via the Internet. The Free Real Estate Office allows sellers to completely handle their own real estate transaction from establishing a price, to advertising, to setting up showings and negotiations. The seller is in control throughout the entire process and closing.

The exact status of your transaction is no longer a mystery.

What a concept! Your property – your transaction – your information!

**To claim your how to, step-by-step free bonus,
simply go to www.FreeRealEstateOffice.com
and enter the code word SHELDON.**

The monologue Multiple Listing Service dinosaur that gives a seller just a one page of property information is now replaced with the dynamic www.FreeRealEstateOffice.com that works in an interactive dialogue format.

There are 3 distinct types of users of the system, each having a differing set of professionals, needs and use for the information. Therefore the three different categories of users each have different offices and information access.

The three different categories of users are:
  -Sellers
  -Buyers and their Agents
  -Negotiators (Sellers and Buyers coming together)

Each of these different users utilizes completely different offices on the site and has access to different information. A separate entry for each office has been established.

Sellers have unrestricted access to the site, utilizing their own specific code to gain full access. At the seller's discretion, this code can be shared with others, perhaps co-owners, partners, children, advisors or attorneys.

After the Offer to Purchase Agreement has been agreed to by all parties, then a more lengthy and formal contract known as The Purchase and Sale Agreement needs to be generated either online from one of the contract suppliers or the Seller's Attorney (**Principal #4**) unless the parties agree to something different. See page 142 for examples of thee contracts.

This agreement needs to be created on the seller's side of the transaction and then downloaded and shared with the buyer's side of the transaction. The time line to execute the Purchase and Sales Agreement is usually done on a fairly tight schedule. The progress of this agreement shall be tracked on the system so that all parties involved will know what action item remains and who is responsible to perform any outstanding issues that block the successful and timely execution of this document. This shall keep everyone's feet to the fire. All parties involved will know exactly who has received the contract and the status of any necessary changes. They will also know who is responsible to make any changes, and in a timely manner, thereby avoiding any unnecessary delays.

First floor

Resource office

- **Pre-Marketing**

    - o Listing desk
    - o Help desk
    - o Pricing and comparables
        - What is on market for like kind properties in area
        - What is sold for like kind properties in area
        - Statistics
            - Average days on market
            - Average per square foot
    - o Disclosure forms
        - Standard
        - Lead paint
        - State required property information
    - o Commission offering
    - o Photography
        - Downloaded
        - Stock

- o Virtual tours
  - ▪ Downloaded
- o Music
  - ▪ By room
  - ▪ Downloaded
  - ▪ Stock
- o Referrals by zip code (3)
  - ▪ Lawyers
  - ▪ Inspection companies
  - ▪ Appraisers
  - ▪ Escrow agents
  - ▪ Engineers
  - ▪ Consultants

Resource Office (continued)

- Property description
- Property features
- Directions and mapping
- Showing instructions
- Higher and better uses
  - o Sub-dividable
  - o Zoning change
  - o Conversions
- Customized links seller selected
  - o Area school rankings
  - o Area recreation
  - o Medical facilities
  - o Colleges
  - o Demographics
  - o Special sites
  - o Blogs
- Printing
  - o Flyers
  - o Handouts
  - o Property information sheets

- o   Inspection reports
- Advertising consultants (optional fee based)
- Free Ebooks

<u>Supply Room</u> Fees apply

- Help desk
- Signage
  - o   FreeREO.com logo, colors, layout
  - o   For sale
  - o   For lease
  - o   Specialty
  - o   Commercial
  - o   Open house
  - o   Directional
- Lock boxes
  - o   Standard
  - o   Electronic downloadable for instant tracking
  - o   Accessible by registered buyer's agents only
- RFID readers
- Printing companies
- Photographers
- Videographers
- Printable forms

<u>Tech Room</u>

- Online classifieds
  - o   Newspaper sites
  - o   Contact info
  - o   Competing sites
  - o   Dates run
  - o   Renewal dates
  - o   Money spent

- o   Type of ad
- Library (snapshot) of other sites utilized
- Listing of other recommended sites (i.e. Trulia.com, Zillow. com, etc.)
- Track hits
- Print advertising and tracking

Communications Office

- Instant notification of buyer interest
- Respond to inquiries
    - o   Phone
    - o   Email
    - o   Text
- Set up showings
    - o   Open houses
- Change/add/update
  Listings
    - o   Links
    - o   Advertising
    - o   Blogs
    - o   Twitter
    - o   Youtube
- History
    - o   Direct buyer showings
    - o   Buyer agent showings
- Property filing cabinet
    - o   Proof of error & omission insurance
        - ▪ Certificates of insurance from
            - Buyer's agents
            - Attorneys
            - Appraisers
            - Consultants
            - Inspection companies
            - Engineers

Information Office

- o Online advice Q&A
- o Local area on line discussion groups (3 zip codes)
  - o Share what's selling
  - o What's working
  - o Who's buying
- o Ratings of area professionals
  - o From previous seller experience
    - Opinions concerning abilities, attitudes, fees and ethics of;
      - Lawyers
      - Inspection companies
      - Realtors
      - Insurance companied
      - Buyers
      - Escrow companies
      - Consultants

  - o Buyer/agent feedback
    - o Provides useable constructive criticism

Fire sale

- o Special section
- o Seller's in trouble can post
- o Must be under priced compared to area market
- o Attempting to inspire quick sale

First floor

Reception

- Help desk

Viewing room

- o See all properties
- o Listings
- o Addresses
- o Prices
- o Photographs
- o Tours
- o Property information
- o Showing instructions
    - Highest and best use for potential changes
        - Sub-dividable
        - Zoning change
        - Conversions

Buyers showing office

- Acknowledge no agent representation
- One time registration for showings
- Showing instructions
- Seller contact information

Buyer's agent showing office

- Register to set up showings
  - o RFID card to use lockboxes
- License number
- Insurance certificate
- Accept commission offering
- Showing instructions

Communications office

- Request additional information
- Receipt of inspection reports
- Submit an offer
- Property feedback, constructive criticism

Match maker/Match maker advertising office

- Fee paid advertising section on www.FreeRealEstateOffice.com
- Buyer's postings of property wanted/needed

SELLER'S OFFICES

Second floor

- o Property filing cabinet
- o Notification of offer received
- o View offer
- o Share offer
- o Email to other decision makers/owners

BUYER'S OFFICES

Second floor

Offer submission office

- Property filing cabinet
- Agreement all offers shall take place on the FreeRealEstateOffice only
- Blank offer forms 3 types
    - o Auto filled in form with information from listing
    - o Boiler plate form, blank for parties to complete
    - o Downloaded custom forms received by email
- All property information
- All inspection reports
- Deposit placement held by
    - o Seller
    - o Seller's attorney
    - o Escrow
    - o Safe Funds
- Execute agreement that the bank and others will provide information to the property filing cabinet in an efficient manner or transaction can be voided by seller
- Submit offer to seller's office.

Conference Room
Negotiating Table

Second floor

o   All offers submitted and negotiated online to this room only. **No exceptions**
o   Changes to offer by both parties until acceptance or rejection
o   Negotiate
    o   Price
    o   Terms
    o   Dates
    o   Deposit amounts
    o   Contingencies
    o   Inspections
    o   Included/excluded in sale
o   Additional provisions
o   Receipt of deposit money
    o   Held by;
        ▪   Seller
        ▪   Seller's attorney
        ▪   Escrow
        ▪   Safe funds
o   Acknowledge receipt by all parties of;

- o Inspection reports
- o Waver of agent representation
  - ▪ Needed from buyer if no agent used
- o Commission offering to agent if involved
- o With Sellers permission live negotiations can take place through seller's attorney
- o Acceptance of offer by all parties
  - o Hard copy by email/mail if necessary.
- o Agreement that all further information generated about transaction or sale;
  - o Becomes the property of the seller
  - o Is shared and sent to property filing cabinet by all
  - o Buyer, vendors and financial institutions are notified and agree to update transaction to property filing cabinet

Third floor

Transaction Department

- o Purchase and Sale Agreement
  - o Example included
  - o Prepared by sellers attorney
  - o Purchased online
  - o Additional deposit
    - To be held in same location as offer deposit
  - o Additional provisions
  - o Track status of purchase and sale agreement
- o Property filing cabinet
  - o All vendors and service providers report and if necessary provide daily update
- o Banks/financial institutions
  - o At buyers direction send loan status update to property filing cabinet
  - o Proof of buyer notification
    - Name
    - Address loan officer or originator

- Contact information including
  - Phone number
  - Email superiors contact information
- Exact loan status
  - Date applied
  - Per-qualified
  - Anticipated commitment date
  - Needed/missing information
  - Key dates, milestones, sink/swim
  - Anticipated closing date
  - Appraisal company and date
    - Notification to send copy of appraisal to property filing cabinet
  - Banks attorney and contact information

Third floor (continued)

Contingency Department

- Performance calendar
  - Generated from offer
  - Updated at purchase and sale agreement
  - Contains all dates and send notifications of all approaching milestones
- Financing
- Permits
  - Occupancy
  - Smoke alarm
  - Lead paint
- Inspections
- Due diligence
  - Land
  - Commercial
  - Municipal approvals
- Automatic closing scheduler with all party notification

Fourth floor

Closing table

o   Attendees

    o   Seller
    o   Seller's attorney
    o   Buyer
    o   Buyer's attorney (if needed)
    o   Buyer's agent (if involved)
    o   Bank or bank's attorney
    o   Escrow company (if needed)
    o   Title company (if needed)

o   Needed

    o   Location and date
    o   Permits
    o   Deed
    o   Property insurance or binder

o   Deposit money
o   Keys
o   Payment of commission
o   Utility transfer
o   Email RESPA to accountants

Unique Features of www.FreeRealEstateOffice.com

Online features:

- Transaction calendar

- Automatic all party closing schedule notification

- Real time financing tracking

- Real time contingency tracking

- Property filing cabinet information sharing

- Instant deposits to bind agreements

- Local referrals of professionals

- Conference room negotiation table

- Comparable/pricing

- Contact with every party involved in the sale or transaction

- Agreement tracking

- Contracts

- Offers

- Ordering

- Feedback from buyers

- Ratings of area professionals

- Information requests

- Ordering of sales materials

- Customizable links by sellers

- Reports

- Scheduling

- Resource room

- Free 12 Sales Principles For Successful Online Property Selling Ebook

- Local Area discussion groups

- Match Maker/Match Maker

- Fire sale

- RESPA for accounting

- Due diligence status

- Multiple access levels for information

Forms and reports:

- Inspections
- Commission agreements
- Property information
- Electronic tracking of showings by agents
- Without agent representation waver
- Proof of insurance certificates
- Offers
- Purchase and Sale
- Closing documents
- Financial Institution full disclosure
- Appraisals

Downloadable printable forms:

- Offers
- Property information sheets
- Mapping
- Commission agreements
- Banking disclosure/ status sharing
- Buyer interest notification
- RESPA (settlement) forms

BUY A SHARE OF THE FUTURE IN YOUR COMMUNITY

These certificates make great holiday, graduation and birthday gifts that can be personalized with the recipient's name. The cost of one S.H.A.R.E. or one square foot is $54.17. The personalized certificate is suitable for framing and will state the number of shares purchased and the amount of each share, as well as the recipient's name. The home that you participate in "building" will last for many years and will continue to grow in value.

Here is a sample SHARE certificate:

HABITAT FOR HUMANITY

THIS CERTIFIES THAT
YOUR NAME HERE
HAS INVESTED IN A HOME FOR A DESERVING FAMILY

1985-2005
TWENTY YEARS OF BUILDING FUTURES IN OUR
COMMUNITY ONE HOME AT A TIME

1200 SQUARE FOOT HOUSE @ $65,000 = $54.17 PER SQUARE FOOT
This certificate represents a tax deductible donation. It has no cash value.

YES, I WOULD LIKE TO HELP!

I support the work that Habitat for Humanity does and I want to be part of the excitement! As a donor, I will receive periodic updates on your construction activities but, more importantly, I know my gift will help a family in our community realize the dream of homeownership. **I would like to SHARE in your efforts against substandard housing in my community!** *(Please print below)*

PLEASE SEND ME _____ SHARES at $54.17 EACH = $ $_____

In Honor Of: _____

Occasion: (Circle One)   HOLIDAY   BIRTHDAY   ANNIVERSARY

OTHER: _____

Address of Recipient: _____

Gift From: _____ *Donor Address:* _____

Donor Email: _____

I AM ENCLOSING A CHECK FOR $ $_____ PAYABLE TO HABITAT FOR HUMANITY OR PLEASE CHARGE MY VISA OR MASTERCARD *(CIRCLE ONE)*

Card Number _____ Expiration Date: _____

Name as it appears on Credit Card _____ Charge Amount $ _____

Signature _____

Billing Address _____

Telephone # Day _____ Eve _____

PLEASE NOTE: Your contribution is tax-deductible to the fullest extent allowed by law.
Habitat for Humanity • P.O. Box 1443 • Newport News, VA 23601 • 757-596-5553
www.HelpHabitatforHumanity.org